DON'T STOP CO$_2$ EMISSIONS!

KEEP BURNING COAL, OIL AND GAS!

CO$_2$ THE GAS OF LIFE

J. C. MIRRE

ISBN: 1500235156
ISBN 13: 9781500235154
Library of Congress Control Number: 2014911235
Createspace Independent publishing Platform
North Charleston, South Carolina

DON'T STOP
CO_2 EMISSIONS!

KEEP BURNING COAL, OIL, AND GAS!

CO_2 THE GAS OF LIFE

Try suggesting that evolution or natural singularities might have a goal or purpose. This idea is an anathema.

The science credo says that evolutionary and physical laws result from random changes and mutations, acts which no force other than natural selection is said to perform.

Any notion of purpose stinks of creationism, while those referring to an "intelligent design" must be considered as the utmost of sacrilege. Anyone blotting his hands with that sort of concept merits the fire curse given to heretics in this material world and the complete obliteration of any traces that might be unearthed from his or her academic records.

THE SAD STORY OF PLANET AZURON

Planet Azuron was nothing but a lifeless globe of ice and snow.

Azuron was first spotted in 2015 by a group of experts at the Ames Center of the Study of Exoplanets (ACSE), a NASA agency dedicated to finding intelligent life outside our solar system.

Azuron belonged to a "solar system" orbiting around the star Tau Ceti. According to data delivered by the Kepler 2 satellite, the basic parameters of the new exoplanet were more than suitable for organic life. Tau Ceti had the same basic constants as our sun, and Azuron was circling its sun in the meso-orbital region: close enough to avoid freezing, but far enough to avoid being scorched.

But there was something strange about Azuron. It was a white, extremely light-reflective planet, and no one could offer an explanation for such a strange oddity. Was it a thick gaseous atmosphere? Or maybe an ice-covered surface or a permanently cloudy surface?

As the years passed, minute amounts of new information slowly trickled in and brought surprising new data. The long list of similarities between Azuron and our Earth grew every year as a result. Having an analogous diameter and mass, the planet rotated on a twenty-five-hour cycle and had an axis tilted twenty degrees to its orbital plane. But that wasn't all: evidence also revealed a thick atmosphere and a strong magnetic field that created an ionospheric mantle that protected the planet's surface from excessive ultraviolet and gamma radiation.

There appeared to be no other essential difference between Azuron and our Earth except the lack of a satellite of its own. Azuron had no moon.

But if Azuron was so similar to Earth, why was it showing such a strong albedo instead of the blue color of our planet? Water should absorb all the blue wavelengths of the light spectra, while continental masses, if present, would show as yellowish-brown smears.

Later on, further images of the new enigmatic planet showed that it wasn't just a speckless white globe after all. A clear yellow-to-reddish band with black spots was seen along the equatorial latitudes, hinting at some time-dependent alterations. The orange colored bands were very slowly changing shapes and somehow moving along, and the black spots would, from time to time, coalesce into bigger ones—or vanish—and then give rise to new and smaller ones. Was it a sign of life?

But until the ExoExplorer50 space probe softly landed on Azuron's surface, those questions remained unanswered. Then in February 2052, the lander deployed its instruments and began transmitting crucial data that helped solve some of the mysteries of Azuron—alas, only to pose new dilemmas.

Azuron was mostly covered by an ice-and-snow carpet of unknown thickness, and its air temperature hovered around zero degrees centigrade at the equator during daylight, dropping to minus fifteen degrees at night. The landing area was swept by strong winds that calmed only very late at night, only to recover after sunrise. Only every now and then—and only for a few weeks in the Azuron year—the air was calm and clear enough so that, under the bright sun, part of the ice and snow cover would melt and form large lakes where dense masses of phytoplankton turned the water a deep bluish-green color. The surrounding icy areas were swiftly covered by extensive colonies of microalgae similar to the earthbound Chlamydomonas nivalis and Chlorococcum infusionum, which are known to stain the ice with a reddish-orange color in glaciers and polar landscapes on our planet. As is well known on Earth, those psychrophile algae rapidly synthesize orange carotenoids that cause the well-known wonders of "red snow," or "blood snow," lowering the water's freezing point and melting it at temperatures below zero degrees centigrade.

But that was not the most astonishing surprise: although the gaseous composition of the Azuron atmosphere was practically the same as Earth's in regard to its nitrogen and oxygen content, there was next to no carbon dioxide—only 100 ppm, or about 0.01 percent!

It was then when the famous geophysicist, Professor Julius Augustus, advanced his theory on the geological history of planet Azuron.

Similar to Earth, the frozen planet would be about five billion years old, and its hot, primitive atmosphere would be made of three main gases: ammonia (NH_3), water vapor, and carbon dioxide (CO_2), with minor oxygen, hydrogen sulfide (SH_2), methane (CH_4), and rare gases. On cooling, water would liquefy and dissolve many of the other gases while filling major depressions and forming oceans. Under such a high-energy environment, the first organic molecules started to form hydrocarbons, amino acids, lipids, and sugars. About one billion years later, the first organized cellules started to multiply and survive thanks to their ability to synthesize hundreds of organic molecules by using water and carbon dioxide as food and sunlight from Tau Ceti as energy through an increasingly dirt-free atmosphere.

These are the very same events that gave rise to life in our own planet. As oxygen was released as a by-product of the photosynthetic process little by little through the eons, atmospheric CO_2 was used to create billons of different organic life-forms and in exchange fill the CO_2-devoid atmosphere with oxygen gas. In other words, the CO_2 gas was transformed into carbon-bearing molecules and solidified in the form of living organisms: viruses, bacteria, algae, pluricellular microorganisms, and complex animals—an incredible and miraculous alchemy!

Soon, the unstoppable process of life started to reduce teratons of CO_2 into cells, tissues, and organs that, once dead, would sink into the ocean's depths, transforming into elementary carbon particles. But the manufacture of organic carbon molecules wasn't the only process to deplete CO_2 from the atmosphere: it was also enhanced by the construction of calcium carbonate tests, at first as the small limestone cells and films on various stromatolite, and later, as all sorts of shells, skeletal frames, crusts, and shields. Through this process, organic carbon-rich tissues and inorganic carbon as carbonates would accumulate as sedimentary rocks or organic-rich formations, such as coal or oil deposits, simple black shale, or carbonaceous particles in sandstones.

Thus began an efficient and irreversible process that depleted carbon dioxide from the atmosphere while increasing its oxygen content at the same time.

Soon, life emerged from the oceans and conquered the continental masses, at first following the same photosynthetic procedure but later as more complex nonautotrophic animal forms that needed plants as food to develop their own cells and inorganic calcium frames.

Obviously, after millions of years of carbon dioxide depletion, the atmosphere became bereft of the vital gas, dropping from a high percentage in the early times to less than 0.1 percent. But even then, millions of tons of carbon dioxide were fixed every year as extensive coral reefs: big rivers carried billions of tons of carbon and organic particles that were buried in marine deltas under meters of fine sediments and clays, forever buried underneath the sea.

By then, Azuron was a planet very similar to today's Earth, with extensive oceans: a full, rich ecosystem: forests: prairies: deserts: snowcapped mountains: rivers: and lakes. And like Earth, all these ecological niches were endowed with all sorts of animals, birds, and insects.

But for some reason, there was no equivalent to our mammalians. Probably because there was never a Chicxulub incident or some other evolution accident, big reptiles were still marauding Azuron's grasslands and swamps. There was no sign of intelligent beings, no transformation of the planet's landscapes. Nothing indicated, at any time, the presence of rational creatures with a capacity to move a stone, raise an earth tumulus, or redesign vegetation communities.

Life continued on its unstoppable tracks for a few more millions years. Very little carbon was allowed to return to the atmosphere, and volcanic activity and biological oxidation processes were simply too meager to compensate for the carbonization of the air.

At first, when CO_2 levels in its atmosphere dropped below 300 ppm, plants started to adapt to the new anoxic situation by increasing the efficiency of their CO_2 absorption. But overall temperatures began to drop, first on polar caps and high latitudes. This somehow reduced the speed of CO_2 depletion by erasing vegetation over vast continental areas.

When CO_2 dropped below 200 ppm, only the most highly adapted plants were able to survive. Complex life-forms and plant-dependent animals were unable to survive. It was very cold for them, and the scarce vegetation was not sufficient for their caloric requirements. Birds and insects, being able to travel for long distances and having well-tuned organs for detecting green areas for feeding, survived over the rest. Carnivores especially were easy prey to the cold, snow, and lack of game—but not for long.

By then, the evolutionary engine kept on creating new, more autotrophic photosynthesizing marine cells that could perfectly survive in such a CO_2-depleted atmosphere. So life, although primitive, went on until CO_2 dropped to 100 ppm.

Then, all life other than microscopic organisms able to thrive under cold conditions and very poor CO_2 atmosphere disappeared.

Only psychrophile algae survived in the equatorial belt, and every now and then, large lakes would form where dense masses of cyanobacteria tainted water in a deep greenish-blue color.

Planet Azuron became a "lifeless" globe of ice and snow.

DON'T STOP
CO_2 EMISSIONS!

KEEP BURNING COAL,
OIL, AND GAS!

CO_2 THE GAS OF LIFE

"The renewal of ice-age conditions would render a large fraction of the world's major food-growing areas inoperable, and so would inevitably lead to the extinction of most of the present human population. Since bolide impacts cannot be called up to order, we must look to a sustained greenhouse effect to maintain the present advantageous world climate.

This implies the ability to inject effective greenhouse gases into the atmosphere, the opposite of what environmentalists are erroneously advocating."

Sir Fred Hoyle and Chandra Wickramasinghe,
Ice, the Ultimate Human Catastrophe (1981)

Summary

The increase of carbon dioxide (CO_2) in the atmosphere is considered a threat to the planet's future, but in fact it should be considered the opposite: the abundance of CO_2 is preventing a looming catastrophe.

This idea might be considered heresy or blasphemy to the present scientific (and almost universal) belief that CO_2 is a poisonous gas that is unavoidably corrupting our atmosphere year after year, leading to what is known as "global warming" or "climate change": a fearful menace to our life, health, and economy.

But if we look beyond the short-term and give pause for thought, we have to admit that CO_2 is not such a poison: in fact, it is the gas of life.

Carbon dioxide is the keystone to the vast biological complex that distinguishes this planet in the solar system and makes it different from the rest: life.

But we are facing a terrific threat: since the beginning of life on Earth about 3.5 billion years ago, the CO_2 content of the atmosphere has been falling a thousand fold from an estimated 40 percent to the current 0.04 percent (400 ppm). And there is no indication that this trend will ever stop. Without human intervention (the burning of fossil fuels), it is bound to fall to 0.03 percent in the very near future, maybe even to 0.02 percent or less. Actually, in the last eight hundred thousand years, it has hovered around those levels on a few occasions, and only twelve thousand years ago (Younger Dryas), it almost caused an irreversible disaster: the end of life on planet Earth.

The real problem is that plants cannot survive at such low atmospheric contents of carbon dioxide, and it is highly probable that below 0.03 percent (300 ppm), most of the vegetation would falter, and as a consequence, all the biological systems on the planet would be put in jeopardy.

There is no reason for the falling CO_2 trend to stop its current decrease down to nearly zero. This is a normal evolutionary process: as the clock ticks, biology changes, the ratios of atmospheric gases change, the planet changes, and the sun changes. The whole universe is in constant change. Humans are the only biological entities capable of halting this tendency toward a CO_2-poor atmosphere, and they can do this by burning the carbon reserves buried in the myriad sedimentary basins around the world.

INTRODUCTION

"What is perhaps most worrying is the increased tendency of pseudoscience in climate research. This is revealed through the bias in publication records toward only reporting results that support one climate hypothesis, while refraining from publishing results that deviate."

Lennart Bengtsson, Senior Research Fellow at the Environmental Systems Science Centre, University of Reading

Carbon dioxide gets truly bad press. It is considered the chief culprit of the "greenhouse effect," the source of the current ongoing climate change. According to the scientific hypothesis in vogue, the exorbitant burning of fossil fuels (coal, oil, and gas) produces vast amounts of CO_2 that scatter through the Earth's atmosphere, increasing its natural content, and jeopardizing life on earth as a result.

As reported by worldwide distributed sensors that measure the atmospheric gases' contents, the amount of carbon dioxide in the air has increased in the past fifty years from an average of 310 ppm to the present 400 ppm. The disturbing fact is that this amount is likely to increase in the future, an unstoppable process that, according to the overwhelming majority of the world scientists, will result in a series of dreadful consequences for the planet's climate and biology, even challenging the future of the human race.

But there is another more important and disregarded fact: 400 ppm isn't a big amount. In fact, if it is written as a percentage, it becomes a more digestible figure: only 0.04 percent of our atmosphere is composed of carbon dioxide.

Furthermore, it is an undeniable fact that our life and all the biology of the planet depend on this minute amount of carbon dioxide.

This gas is essential to the life of plants, which are the very bases of all trophic chains. They are the key to life on the planet.

No plants can live without carbon dioxide.

No animals can live without plants.

No human beings can live without plants.

What would happen if the world's scientific consensus is wrong and suddenly finds that, although human industry is guilty of the last two hundred years of increases in carbon dioxide, CO_2 levels have actually been *diminishing* for the last 3.5 billion years?

Such a trend in depletion could exhaust our carbon dioxide in a very near future. In this situation, the amount of this vital gas will be so low that plants will stop growing, reproducing, and feeding us.

This possibility is not science fiction. This possibility is not the result of a catastrophic event with a very low statistical probably, such as a big asteroid strike. Neither is an extremely remote certitude.

It is there, it is the final outcome of a process that started 3.5 billion years ago—the same process that created the oxygen that we breathe, the oceans we enjoy in summertime, and the water we drink from springs and rivers. All natural processes have a starting point and an ending stage. Biology and life started on the surface of our planet 3.5 billion years ago, and someday this marvelous alchemy is bound to finish.

That is an inescapable certitude. An inconvenient truth.

Humanity cannot escape from this basic rule.

But human beings are smart enough and capable of extending the deadline further into the future, reducing its effects, and making things a little bit easier.

But let us start from the beginning.

CONTENTS

CHAPTER 1:

SOME BASIC FIGURES AND CONCEPTS

Teleology

The study of evidences of design in nature – A doctrine (as in vitalism) that ends are immanent in nature – A doctrine explaining phenomena by final causes – The fact or character attributed to nature or natural processes of being directed toward an end or shaped by a purpose – The use of design or purpose as an explanation of natural phenomena

Merriam-Webster Dictionary

Most of the books published on the "CO_2 saga" or the "CO_2 religion" refer to the history of the atmospheric content of CO_2 during the last three hundred years, typically comparing what has been established as the "preindustrial" level or content, with dates for that era ranging between 1750 and 1800. Some authors, and in particular those referring to the ice core data obtained from numerous drill sites on both the Arctic and Antarctic ice caps, would rather extend their reasoning back to eight hundred thousand years before the present.

In this book, we will talk about the whole history of CO_2 in our planet from the very beginning of life—or 3.5 billion years before the present. For the sake of simplicity, we shall use the following abbreviations:

YBP = years before present
MYBP = million years before present
BYBP = billion years before present

As we will refer to studies based on the geological history of our planet, we thought it would be useful and practical to provide a summary in the following Table, a highly simplified geological time scale.

As we are using a number of calculations, transforming amounts of CO_2 in the atmosphere, and sometimes the equivalent carbon content, it will be useful to recap some basic figures:

1 ton (metric) of CO_2 = 556 m^3 (cubic meters), or 556,200 liters of CO_2.

Amounts of CO_2 gas in the atmosphere are either given as a percentage (%) or as parts per million (ppm):

1% = 10,000 ppm 1,000 ppm = 0.1%

In other calculations, the following contents are used:

Carbon (C) content of CO_2 = 28%
Calcium-rich limestone content in CO_2 = 44%
Carbon content in calcium-rich limestone = 12%

Some mass or weight figures:
Tons are always expressed as metric tons (tm):

1,000 t or Kt = 1×10^3 tm
1,000,000 t or Mt = 1×10^6 tm
1 billion t or Gt = 1×10^9 tm
1 trillion t or Tt = 1×10^{12} tm
1 petaton = 1×10^{15} tm

1Tcf of natural gas = 1 trillion cubic feet of natural gas

TABLE 1. ELEMENTARY GEOLOGICAL TIME SCALE

EON/ERA	PERIOD	EPOCH	MYBP
	Quaternary (2.6	Holocene	10,000 YBP to present
	MYBP to present)	Pleistocene	2.6 to 0.01 (10,000 YBP)
CENOZOIC	Neogene (5 MYBP	Pliocene	Ends at 2.6
	to 2.6 MYBP)	Miocene	Ends at 5
	Paleogene 66 to	Oligocene	Ends at 25
	5 MYBP	Eocene	Ends at 34
		Paleocene	Ends at 57
MESOZOIC	Cretaceous		Ends at 66
	Jurassic		Ends at 140
	Triassic		Ends at 192
PALEOZOIC	Permian		Ends at 235
	Carboniferous		Ends at 290
	Devonian		Ends at 365
	Silurian		Ends at 411
	Ordovician		Ends at 440
	Cambrian		Ends at 505
PROTEROZOIC			2,500 to 570
ARCHEAN EON			4,000 to 2,500
HADEAN EON			4,567 to 4,000

CHAPTER 2:

PLANTS, THE FACTORIES THAT CHANGE A CHEAP GAS INTO SOLID RICHES

"We believe Earth and its ecosystems—created by God's intelligent design and infinite power and sustained by His faithful providence—are robust, resilient, self-regulating, and self-correcting, admirably suited for human flourishing, and displaying His glory. Earth's climate system is no exception. Recent global warming is one of many natural cycles of warming and cooling in geologic history."

Cornwall Alliance's Evangelical Declaration on Global Warming

As we all know, plants on the land and algae in the oceans (including photosynthesizing bacteria) are the only living creatures on the planet that are able to synthesize their own food from three simple, basic elements: air, water, and sunlight. Those biological entities capable of accomplishing such a miraculous alchemy have a special name: **autotrophs**—from the Greek words *auto* (self) and *throphos* (eating).

Why is this a miraculous alchemy?

Because plants are able to transform something invisible, shapeless, and immaterial like the light of sun and air into a three-hundred-foot sequoia tree with just the help of a little water.

Consider the Amazonian forests, the African jungles, the Siberian taiga (millions of square miles carpeted with a dense population of pine trees), and the never-ending flatlands of grasses, mosses, and lichens of the northern Canadian and Siberian tundras. In these areas, about one teraton (10^{12} tons) of organic vegetal matter is continuously growing, dying, and renewing almost every year. On top of it, we must add another teraton of carbon locked in organic, plant-related matter, so that some 2×10^{12} metric tons of carbon belong to living vegetable tissue on our planet via the exclusive sources of air, water, and light.

But this mind-blowing wonder is not restricted to the continental masses. It is also happening in the seas and oceans that make up about 70 percent of the Earth's surface, which hold many more teratons of live organic matter in the form of algae and bacteria, extending from the oceans' surfaces to almost a thousand feet deep, down to the fathoms where the sun's light fades into darkness.

Using simple words, we can say that plants, algae, and other autotrophs are just transforming machines that change shapeless gases and liquids into a growing, living entity that never stops working: *life.*

Moreover, plants and algae have the ability to synthesize thousands of different molecules, from simple sugars and acids to more complex fats and amino acids, and further still to extremely complex proteins and nucleic acids. Strangely enough, some of those molecules are ubiquitous, which means that the same substances are found in extremely different organisms, including some proteins that are found in wheat grains, whale skin, eagles' feathers, and microscopic amoeba. Glucose, for instance, is a simple sugar that makes up part of the organic complexity of millions of different beings.

But the key argument is the fact that all non-plant-related beings, from the smallest insect to humans, rely on plants for their survival. Trees, grass, and algae are able to manufacture the millions of chemical molecules that they use for their own tissues, growth, and reproduction, while most of those same molecules are the basic nutrients that animals use to build and preserve their own cells.

With the exception of some bacteria, fungi, and archaea that thrive by chemosynthesis—that is, obtaining their necessary carbon from methane or other carbonaceous compounds and using different sources of energy instead of the sun's light—plants and algae are the very starting point for all trophic chains.

THE CHERNOBYL MUSHROOM

An atomic reactor the Ukrainian Chernobyl Nuclear Power Plant melted down in April, 1986. In a matter of a few days, the nearby town of the same name, population fifty thousand, was totally evacuated; the fission chamber was later covered by massive loads of concrete slabs intended for the isolation of the reactor from the surrounding environment. Since then, and now for almost thirty years since, a rounded area of sixty kilometers diameter (an area of 1,100 square miles, twice the expanse of New York City) was declared a "no-man's-land" or "exclusion zone," where only a limited number of workers are allowed to enter to measure fallout and for decontamination and remediation.

In 2007, Russian technicians sent a robot into the darkness of the failed reactor, where deadly radiation ten thousand times the standard normal background was measured. No life was deemed possible under such conditions, and any human venturing into the reactor would have died of deadly contamination within a few minutes. But there was a surprise at the very core of the reactor: its walls were plastered with a thick mass of black molds. How was it possible for a fungus to grow and multiply in such an eerie ecosystem?

A second revelation soon followed: the molds were not exceptional but rather a common type of mushroom called *Cryptococcus neoformans,* a widespread and well-known mold. In this case, there was a third shocker: the fungus was a peculiar type of *C. neoformans,* containing high amounts of melanin. Normal *C. neoformans* doesn't have melanin pigment, but it starts producing this substance when subjected to intense radiation. This black melanin molecule plays the role of the chlorophyll pigment in plants and absorbs the ionizing radiation's energy instead of the sun's light to provide the fungus with the energy to synthesize the necessary organic molecules for life. So, the radioactive variety of C. neoformans thrives in the darkness using gamma radiation as an energy source and carbon from both atmospheric CO_2 and the abandoned graphite rods used for the reactor's cooling.

Curiously, researchers E. Dadachova and A. Casadevall (2008), both experts on this kind of mushroom, noticed that highly melanized fungal spores were found in the Cretaceous/Tertiary boundary, an era that coincided with the famous Chicxulub event.

According to orthodox scientific belief, melanin is considered a skin pigment that protects us from UV radiation, but no explanation is given for its role in the brain, the digestive epithelium, the bone marrow, the adrenal glands, and many other organs. The photoelectric properties of melanin, specifically its capacity to generate free electrons and water dissociation when struck with either light or any other shorter wave radiation (as in the case of the Chernobyl mushrooms), have been known for half a century, and researchers like Dr. B. J. Nicolaus (2005) propose that melanin acts as a modulator or enhancer of nervous transmission, blocking the reversing effect of the electrical impulse.

Plants make most of the carbohydrates, fats, and proteins (amino acids) that we know of, as well as essential vitamins, enzymes, and organo-mineral complexes.

Plants are the envy of the chemical industry and energy experts. Their effectiveness in harnessing sunlight and transforming water and CO_2 from the air into millions of organic chemical substances does not compare to the huge human-made chemical factories that inefficiently produce only a few compounds, wasting huge amounts of energy and water in the process. Chlorophyll is the key enzymatic material that allows the chemical transformation of solar photons into millions of different CHON (**carbon, hydrogen, oxygen** and **nitrogen**) molecules.

WE TOO ARE BASICALLY MADE OF CO_2 AND WATER

In the case of human beings, for every two hundred atoms that make up our organic constitution, 126 (63 percent) are hydrogen atoms, fifty-one (26 percent) are oxygen, nineteen (10 percent) are carbon, three are nitrogen (1.5 percent), and one atom per two hundred are others (basically calcium, phosphorus and potassium).

Considering the atomic mass instead of these atoms, the results are quite different: we are made of 65 percent oxygen, 18.5 percent carbon, 9.5 percent hydrogen, and 3 percent nitrogen. The rest being mainly calcium (1.5 percent), phosphorus (1 percent), potassium (0.4 percent), sulfur (0.3 percent), and sodium (0.2 percent).

In fact, we are made by some 70 percent water and 25 percent CO_2, with the remaining 5 percent comprising salts such as chlorides, phosphates, and sulfates of calcium, sodium, and potassium.

In a sense, plants live on air. Thus, sugars and fats are produced through the moisture in the air, specifically the oxygen and carbon from the carbon dioxide content in the atmosphere. Some of those plants are even able to make use of atmospheric nitrogen to produce proteins.

CHAPTER 3:

THE ESSENTIALS WE LEARNED AT SCHOOL

"The global warming alarm movement appears to be the latest manifestation of a common social phenomenon: false alarms based on unscientific forecasts of human-caused environmental disasters."

The global warming alarm: Forecasts from the structured analogies method - Kesten C. Green, Scott Armstrong 2007

No life is possible without sunlight.

Sunlight is essential to put into motion the colossal thermal machine that generates the global climate. Without solar heat, there would be neither wind nor humidity to produce clouds and perpetuate the water cycle. But in addition, from a biological point of view, no one can deny the essential character of sun for life, and in particular for the survival of plants that need sunlight's energy to synthesize all the organic compounds needed for their growth and development.

No life is possible without water.

Life on the planet began 3.5 billion years ago in the primitive ocean waters, and living organisms didn't manage to conquer the emerging lands until three billion years later. As René Quinton (1904) remarked more than a century ago, life on dry lands mimics marine life, and continental plant and animal cells are basically made of salty water, the same salts that were dissolved in the primitive oceans.

THE WEATHER-MAKING BACTERIA AND THE ATMOSPHERIC MICROBIOME

A few years ago, a number of researchers from the Georgia Institute of Technology, in collaboration with NASA, started a program to collect airborne bacteria. According to N. DeLeon-Rodriguez et al. (2013), bacteria represent 20 percent of the 0.25–1 micron particles at thirty thousand feet above both cloudy and clear skies before, during, or after major Caribbean hurricanes. More than twenty different taxa of bacteria and minor fungal cells with an average concentration of 4,250 organisms per cubic foot were recognized by the use of PCR (polymerase chain reaction) techniques, and most of which were able to survive at minus thirty-five to forty-five degrees centigrade by metabolizing carbon compounds present in the atmosphere. The main families recognized were *Methylobacteriaceae* and *Oxalobacteraceae*, which are both capable of metabolizing oxalic acid, one of the most abundant organic acids in the atmosphere. Another feature of these atmospheric bacterial colonies is that they change according to the geographical situation on land, since they are basically freshwater and soil bacteria hovering above continental areas and marine-dwelling bacteria in the oceans.

But the most relevant climate issue is the ability of these bacteria to effectively become nuclei for the formation of water droplets and ice crystals. The fact that about 85 percent of the known taxa belong to aquatic bacteria well-known for their efficiency in forming nuclei underscores the importance of the atmospheric microbiome as a dynamic climate control factor.

Due to their larger size and surface area, rainmaking bacteria are more efficient than inert particles at forming water or ice nuclei, their main advantage being that some of these microbes can form ice crystals at several degrees above zero centigrade. *Pseudomonas syringae* is well-known for its ability to form snow at warmer temperatures some degrees above water's freezing point—a reason for its use at sky resorts!

This bacterium and other similar ones have special proteins in their cell membranes called INA (Ice Nucleation Active) proteins. According to B. C. Christner et al. (2008), these rainmaking bacteria are found worldwide, from the tropics to Antarctica, but their importance as weather or climatic control agents hasn't been gauged yet.

Janine Fröhlich-Nowoisky et al. (2009) from the Max Planck Institute for Chemistry in Germany have found that *P. syringae* proteins are capable of ordering the surrounding water molecules in such a way that, structurally speaking, they are almost ice crystals at several degrees above zero degrees centigrade. But the most surprising fact is that those proteins are not exclusive of *P. syringae*, since other bacteria and even some fungal spores have airborne ice-nucleating capacity.

Since these microorganisms have the potential to influence weather patterns, the question arises as to what extent life was contributing to the past climate changes and evolution, and to what extent they contribute to the formation of a desert or a tropical jungle.

RED RAINS OR BLOOD RAINS

Although noticed and recorded since the beginning of historical records, the red-colored rains were rarely studied until the present, despite being quite a widespread and universal wonder. Recently this phenomenon was particularly frequent in the region of Kerala, India, with events in 2001, 2006, 2007, 2008 and 2012. According to a study by S. Sampath et al. (2001) on that year event the water tainting organisms were identified as the algal spores of *Trentepohlia* (a genus of terrestrial algae that thrives on rocky surfaces or tree bark, often by itself and also as part of lichens' symbiotic associations) probably one of many other water tainting organisms. The orange-reddish color is due to a high carotenoid content that hides the green chlorophyll. Spores of these algae are stocked in filaments of less than a micron in diameter that can be easily blown up to tropospheric altitudes where they become ice nucleation active, coloring the resultant water droplets.

But below the cellular level, the bases of biology are the millions of CHON compounds that are dissolved in an aqueous vehicle together with inorganic salts. Some of the water required by plants for the biosynthesis of complex organic molecules is provided by the air's humidity. However, that amount is insufficient, since, in their evolution, plants developed special physiological mechanisms enabling them to absorb the water retained in soils through their roots and profit from the minerals dissolved in the moist soil.

No life is possible without CO_2.

As is the case with sun and water, plants need the CO_2 contained in the air to make the millions of organic molecules that involve carbon as the fundamental frame element. It is well-known that *life is essentially the biology of carbon.*

This means that the CO_2 from the atmosphere is extremely important for life on the planet, as are sun and water.

Therefore, it follows that if there was no CO_2 in the atmosphere, plants wouldn't be able to synthesize organic compounds. They wouldn't be able to produce sugars, fats, proteins, or vitamins.

On the other hand, there is no way to substitute the atmospheric CO_2 as a carbon source to synthesize all the organic molecules that make the basis of life. Plants cannot absorb carbon from the soils, nor can they take up the carbon from limestone or the organic matter resulting from the decay of other plants or animals (carnivorous plants benefit only from the proteins and minerals of insects, not their sugars or fats).

The unique carbon-bearing compound that plants can use is the CO_2 contained in the atmosphere. The capacity of plants to synthesize the myriad organic molecules depends on the availability of this gas.

And if for some reason this CO_2 atmospheric resource becomes unavailable, then plants wouldn't survive. And without plants, neither animals nor human beings would survive.

Why?

Because of evolution.

Thousands of books discuss the aspects, questions, doubts, and theories of life's evolution, the evolution of organic beings. But very few consider evolution as a whole process, a unidirectional chain of events that started eons before the appearance of organic life on Earth.

That is, an inorganic evolution: our cosmos, our star, and our moon, together with our home planet, all followed a chain of events or sequential processes.

One of the consequences of a thick atmosphere containing a 40-percent CO_2 concentration as our planet started to cool around 4 BYBP was the organization of the first organic carbon molecules in the primitive seas.

The Earth is endowed with complex organic life because carbon was abundantly available in both the atmosphere and in the lukewarm waters of the primitive seas.

What an irony!

The despised, loathed carbon dioxide gas, that many consider a poison, that massive numbers of scientists consider the root of our planet-dooming climate change…is the very basis of life.

We are made of carbon dioxide, we come from carbon dioxide, and without carbon dioxide we cannot live.

We all rely on such a tiny amount!

It seems hard to believe, but life on the planet depends on the tiny amount (0.04 percent) of carbon dioxide contained in the earth's atmosphere, a minute volume.

For those familiar with the metric scale, 0.04 percent of a meter is less than half a millimeter.

Zero point zero four percent of a full day is only about thirty seconds.

For an eighty-year lifespan, 0.04 percent is only eleven days—maybe the happiest days in your life: your first holydays to Florida, your honeymoon in Paris...

Flying from New York to Paris takes seven hours, forty-six minutes; 0.04 percent of that time is barely what you spend fastening your seat belt: eleven seconds.

According to the US Department of Agriculture, 2,640 calories is the average daily adult food intake. Of that, 0.04 percent is the caloric intake of the unsweetened espresso you sip as you finish your lunch.

On Mount McKinley, 0.04 percent of its altitude (20,236 feet) is eight feet, a few inches more than the tallest ever NBA player in its history at seven feet, seven inches.

The total area of Rhode Island (1,545 square miles) is about 0.04 percent of the total area of the United States (3,803,290 square miles).

If we use climatology as a comparative scale, we will be surprised to learn that 0.04 percent of the average yearly rainfall in the Amazonian tropical forest (two thousand millimeters) is the yearly amount of rain in the Atacama Desert (one millimeter), the driest desert on the planet.

Two thousand and fourteen years have elapsed since Jesus's birth; 0.04 percent of the history of Christendom is less than a year's time: only ten months.

Malcom Cecil-Cockwell makes an interesting comparison in his book *Objective Ecology* (2007), which inspired the following:

The total volume of Earth's atmosphere can fit in 104 cases of twenty-four twelve-ounce beer cans. That makes for a total of 2,496 beer cans, which is enough booze to drink about seven cans a day throughout the year. The atmospheric carbon dioxide content in this context would be equivalent to one single can.

CHAPTER 4:

THE NATURAL CO₂ DEPLETION

"The basic greenhouse effect is good: if the atmosphere did not contain greenhouse gases, the average temperature on the Earth would be approximately 59°F colder, and it is unlikely that life as we know it would be able to exist."

COOL IT - Bjorn Lomborg

It is a well-established fact that, over the last 3.5 billion years, the carbon dioxide contained in our Earth's atmosphere has been decreasing. No one doubts it, and it is considered an undeniable fact.

Although preceded by other authors, Alan J. Kaufman and Shuhai Xiao (2003) published a paper in *Nature* that established that the carbon dioxide in the atmosphere in the early Archean was somewhere between 22 and 40 percent. They were also the first to realize that the carbon dioxide content in the earth's atmosphere dropped about a thousand times since then to the current concentration of 0.04 percent.

What the scientific community doesn't seem to realize is that this depletion is a one-way process, and there is no reason or accident that would stop its course.

The natural course is that carbon dioxide is decreasing, and it will continue to do so in the future. Sooner or later, we could be facing a risky scenario in which the carbon dioxide concentration fall below 200 ppm in our planet's atmosphere.

FIGURE 1. DECREASE OF ATMOSPHERIC CO$_2$ SINCE 3.5 BYBP

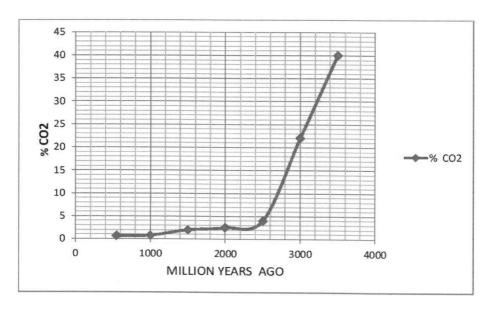

The figure above (based on Kaufman's [2003] data, with a slight simplification) shows the decline of the atmospheric CO$_2$ content since 3.5 BYBP.

This decline is quite obviously due to the continuous gobbling of atmospheric CO$_2$ by cyanobacteria first (in the Precambrian) and algae and other photosynthesizing organisms later. Finally—once plants conquered the landmasses—the CO$_2$ withdrawal machine attained the summit of perfection.

But as we considered above, CO$_2$ wasn't solely integrated as organic tissues, but also by all sorts of calcareous shells and shields, from microscopic stromatolitic bacteria to the metric sizes of the South Pacific giant clams like *Tridacna gigas* and other species.

TRIDACNA GIGAS

This creature is the largest living mollusk, measuring up to fifty-six inches (1.4 meters) in length and more than 450 pounds (about two hundred kilos) in weight. It is normally found in the Pacific Coral Seas and more sparsely in the equatorial waters between the East African Coast and the South China Sea. Its tremendous size and accelerated growth rate are related to a very strange and exceptional phenomena: they feed like normal mollusks, filtering plankton and microorganisms dispersed in the nutrient-poor coral reef environment, but they also metabolize CO_2 and make their own sugars using a symbiotic algae that is incorporated into its mantle called zooxanthellae.

In fact, this clam cultivates an inner orchard of unicellular algae that produces sugars for both, while the surrounding seaweed also profits in the presence of other metabolic waste products produced by the clam. This translates into a growth rate of half an inch per year and a hundred years of live—plus an extraordinary concentration of carbon dioxide in the shells.

Curiously, this clam is considered a gourmet delicacy in many countries, while the Chinese believe its flesh to be an aphrodisiac. This may not be too far from reality, given its high zinc, aspartic acid, and methyl-D-aspartate contents. These two last amino acids have been shown to be testosterone boosters, while zinc has been successfully employed against male infertility and sexual dysfunction.

Incidentally, *Tridacna* is small compared to the nine-foot-round *Platyceramus platinus,* a Late Cretaceous giant clam that dwelled in the Colorado Niobrara shale and limestone (famous today for its rich oil shale and gas shale horizons). It was probably very different to *Tridacna* since its habitat constituted anoxic inland and brackish seawaters. Actually, the Cretaceous (80 MYBP) was most probably the geological period when life produced the most gigantic animals and plants—doing so on a scale quite similar to the extremely large ferns that grew during the Carboniferous days (300 MYBP).

Although they are typical seawater mollusks, some oyster species choose brackish waters as their preferred habitat. Oysters are an example of animals that have retained their physical appearance, physiology, and ecological niche without major changes (even as pearl makers since the Triassic [250 MYBP]). The Austrian village of Stetten (in the wine area of Korneuburg, some ten miles north of Vienna) is famous for its layers of fossilized Miocene (16 MYBP) oysters beds, where several specimens attain lengths of three feet and weights of more than twenty pounds.

If we now look closely at Figure 1, we can see that many eons before that, when life started in the primitive oceans some 3.5 billion years ago, the atmospheric CO_2 content was probably around 40 percent.

Although there is no total agreement in the scientific community, one has to face the fact that never before in the last 3.5 billion years was the Earth's biology challenged by such an appalling shrinking of the CO_2 content in the atmosphere. There is no evidence in the fossil record indicative of a period in the past when the CO_2 contained in the Earth's atmosphere was lower that 0.04 percent, with the sole exception of the recent glacial intervals in the last eight hundred thousand years.

About 3.5 BYBP, something new emerged on the planet Earth that changed the old geochemistry of atmosphere and oceans: **LIFE.**

Carbon dioxide began to be sequestered by organisms under the form of both elemental carbon (forming organic molecules) and $CaMgCO_3$ (as calcareous shells and crusts of marine invertebrates), and carbon was thus removed from the atmosphere and exchanged for the oxygen that those same organisms started to produce as a metabolic end product.

Most authors dedicate extensive articles and experiments trying to understand and explain the equilibrium between atmospheric CO_2 and the gas dissolved in oceanic waters—and in particular the ratio between the acidity or alkalinity of the seas' waters and its relation to the atmospheric concentration of CO_2. All those experiments and considerations are based on pure chemical reactions between atmospheric CO_2 and its dissolution in water. But they never (or rarely) consider life as part of the equation. This is a great mistake, since life-forms can easily reduce the CO_2 contained in oceanic waters by either organic matter sequestration or via organic (protein-bonded) carbonate fixation.

The tendency to ignore the main role of life in geological processes (nonigneous) is widespread. Evaporites, for instance, are studied as the simple result of the chemistry of salt concentrations, ionic solubility, and temperatures of restricted aquatic conditions, such as sabkhas or brackish lagoon environments. Only a very selective minority of earth scientists are questioning whether extremophiles couldn't exert a much greater influence in their capacity to alter the chemical balances in their environments than the assumed figures deduced from pure chemical solutions experiments that don't consider the potential effects of life's transforming capabilities.

Moreover, there is a persistent and worldwide association between organic-rich sediments with evaporites, and more specifically between oil deposits and evaporitic basins. The repeated coincidence of these two events is found at different times all along geological history, from the Proterozoic to the present. It is also a well-known fact that bacteria and other microorganisms can massively transform sulfates (S^{+6}) into elemental sulfur (S^0) or sulfides (S^{-2}) in a given environment, while other organisms can change water's pH or redox conditions by reducing or oxidizing anions such as Fe or N, similar to their capacity to fix or free carbon and oxygen.

Annex I discusses the implications of biology and geology with the current "ocean acidification" dupe.

Another example of life being ignored by geochemists and the like is shown in papers devoted to the study of rock weathering. Weathering is *not* the result of atmospheric and water chemistry by which the solubility of the ions of rock-forming minerals can be calculated *exclusively* considering physical variables like temperature, a reducing or oxidizing atmosphere, or the partial pressure of dissolved CO_2 in water.

Biological constraints and *not* the pure chemistry of ionic solubility are the driving factors. Soils are the weathering process media, and the soil's biome has far more important consequences than whatever can be gathered by the chemistry of simple water-gas-ionic dilutions. A soil is an active biological ecosystem where fungus mycelium (mycorrhizae) and bacteria (some nitrifying, others denitrifiers, etc.) are hundreds or thousands times more active chemical exchangers and catalyzers than just the studied simple chemical changes of ion solubility in water. The amount of oxygen or CO_2 dissolved in the soil is irrelevant when compared to the biochemical action of the soil microbiome. The intensity and depth of the weathering crust depends on the biological activity and the symbiotic relationships between plants and the microbial ecosystem. The degree of weathering is more a result of soil's biological activity than temperature or amount of dissolved gases in the soils' water.

Lichens make an outstanding example of the importance of biological activity in regards to weathering intensity.

LICHENS: THE PIONEERS

In their book *Lichens of North America* (2001), authors I. M. Brodo et al. consider lichens "nature's pioneers" due to their ability to colonize bare rock surfaces, much to the chagrin of experts in monument deterioration and conservation. Fungal hyphae can penetrate through mineral fractures several millimeters in depth and thus increase the action of organic acids (e.g., depsides, depsidones, oxalic) over reactive surfaces to make the rock-forming minerals more soluble. It must be stressed that lichens can withstand long periods of drought, and on top of it, some species incorporate cyanobacteria with nitrogen-fixing capacities.

This was also mentioned by Stretch and Viles (2002) in an article about lichens that grew on lava flows that

erupted almost three centuries ago in the Canary
Islands, developing a weathered crust 0.25 millimeters (0.01 inches) thick, compared to only 0.01 millimeters thick on bare rock surfaces unspoiled by lichens.
Nevertheless, the authors remark that similar studies in
Hawaiian lavas show weathering crusts of up to 1.5 millimeters thick and up to a hundredfold wider that on
non-lichen-colonized surfaces.

FIGURE 2. DECREASE OF THE ATMOSPHERIC CO_2 SINCE 550 MYBP

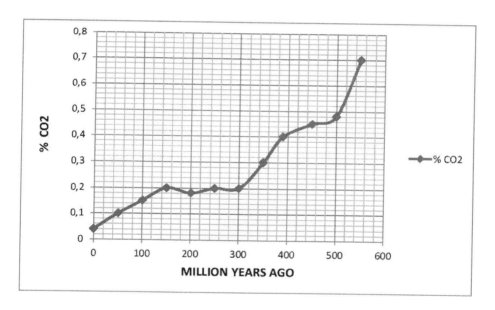

Figure 2 shows the decrease of atmospheric CO_2 since the
Cambrian (550 MYBP) and its gradual fall to the present level according to GEOCARB III (Berner and Kothavala 2001). In this data, we are
assuming the upper limit of Berner's (2001) estimation of about 0.2
percent CO_2 (2,000 ppm) content in the Carboniferous air, some three
hundred million years ago.

As is shown in the figure, during the Cambrian explosion (541
MYBP), the CO_2 content of atmosphere was estimated as 0.7 percent,
almost twenty times today's average.

Marine life was burgeoning in those days, and apparently neither trilobites nor graptolites were at all affected by the oceans' acidity. Moreover, evidence of reef construction can be found all over the world (Hicks and Rowland 2004, 2009), such as in Morocco, the United States, the Yukon, Sardinia, Mexico, Iran, Australia, and China. Also, extensive and thick algal limestone deposits accumulated in the Cambrian seas from Jordan's Dead Sea to the Appalachian Mountains. Perhaps in those days there were no climate change scientists like I. Cripps et al. (2011) or P. L. Munday et al. (2012) to warn them against dwelling in such corrosive waters.

A FEW WORDS ABOUT THE ALLEGED CARBONIFEROUS GLACIATION

Berner and Kothavala (2001), as well as other researchers, sustain the argument that during the Upper Carboniferous and Lower Permian (about 300 MYBP), the average CO_2 content of the atmosphere was close to the present level (about 350 ppm). But this hypothesis needs to be seriously reconsidered, since that period was one of the spells in the Earth's geological history when organic matter productivity was at its peak, not only as witnessed by the massive volumes of coal beds and organic-rich sediments that were produced by lavish vegetation, but also through the huge deposits of calcium carbonate made by coral reefs, limestone layers, and calcareous sediments built by carbonate shells bearing organisms and microorganisms that required an abundant supply of calcium ions delivered to the oceans by acidic rivers rich in dissolved CO_2. A very recent and astounding example of an Early Permian (295 MYBP) hot and humid climate was the unearthing of the perfectly preserved forest in a Mongolian coal mine described by Wang and Pfefferkorn (2012). Many Permian and Triassic sedimentary basins have been thoroughly studied in Australia that show thousands of meters of carbon-rich black shale, coal measures, oil shale, limestone and evaporites layers, all undeniable indicators of warm climatic conditions.

Warren (2006) refers to several gigantic evaporite basins in the Carboniferous age in the St. Lawrence Gulf, where they reach a thickness of up to 16,500 feet. In the Permian, one has to mention the extensive Zechstein evaporites extending over most of Northern Europe and the North Sea. But Permian and Lower Triassic evaporites are also found in the Amazon, the famous Delaware, other Permian basins in Texas, and the more famous Khuff anhydrite beds of the Persian Gulf and Oman.

There is a lot of confusion regarding the atmospheric CO_2 content and the so-called "widespread continental glaciations." In the Royer (2006) paper, it is suggested that a threshold below 1,000 ppm will trigger so-called "continental glaciations." This is a rather a bizarre statement, considering that currently we are not witnessing any continental glaciation, with the exception of Greenland and Antarctica, which are rather relics of a late continental-scale glaciation. Applying the old principle that the present is the key to the past, the current global situation is one of coetaneous, thick, and extensive ice masses that were built up over the polar caps (able to form outstanding tillite deposits not very far from the polar circles), while at the same time, evaporitic deposits and carbon-rich sediments are piling up in the tropics. This could easily explain the coexistence of tillite with coal measures, evaporites, and coral reefs during the Upper Carboniferous, Permian, and Triassic—keeping in mind that CO_2 levels in those days were clearly above the 1,000 ppm threshold, not below.

But the most puzzling and nonsensical situation is the rapid (thin) lateral or world vertical transition between the Dwyka tillite and the thick coal deposits with billions of tons reserves found in South Africa. Are the so-called Dwyka tillite real glacial debris accumulations? Couldn't the Dwyka beds be better explained as apron mudflow deposits, not implying continental ice masses?

Coal measures in South Africa develop in lateral continuity to the so-called Dwyka tillite in the early Permian. The Gondwana coal deposits of Africa and elsewhere are characterized by the remnants of the rich *Glossopteris* and *Gangamopteris* flora that extend from the Permian well into the Triassic.

The BP Statistical Review of World Energy (2013) estimates the current South African coal reserves as 76 Gtm (0.076×10^{12} tm), Australian coal reserves at 76 Gtm, and Indian coal reserves 60 Gtm. These more-than-two-hundred Gtm of coal are measured reserves, that is, coal that can be extracted and sold at the current market conditions. But if other unknown or uncalculated resources are considered (Brazil, Antarctica, and other African countries) it is highly possible that Gondwana coal seams and carbon-rich shale reach at least one teratons (10^{15} tm).

Furthermore, and as we shall explain later on, a 350 ppm CO_2 atmosphere hypothesis is in conflict with the onset of C_4 plants, a radical change that enhanced the photosynthesizing power of new plants, an event that took place much later in the Miocene (10 MYBP), when the CO_2 atmospheric content was below 0.1 percent (1,000 ppm).

Later, in the middle Paleozoic, coral reefs developed so massively that they built up many of today's mountains in different areas of the planet, apparently unaffected and undisturbed by such sea-acidification phenomena as those claimed by G. De'ath et al. (2009) and other climate change doomsters that use similar arguments. If those scientists are correct and corals today are in danger because a 0.04-percent CO_2 concentration in the air, how is it that corals were covering millions of square miles of oceanic waters when the atmospheric CO_2 content in the Devonian atmosphere was ten times the present (around 0.4 percent)?

A few million years after, at the end of the Cretaceous, when the last happy *Ankylosaurus* and other fellow herbivorous dinosaurs were grazing over probably the first prairies on the face of Earth, CO_2 had already dwindled to a mere 0.1 percent (still more than twice the present ratio).

CHAPTER 5:

WHERE HAS ALL THAT 40 PERCENT CO$_2$ ATMOSPHERIC CARBON GONE?

"Science is a very successful way of knowing, but not the only way. We acquire knowledge in many other ways, such as through literature, the arts, philosophical reflection, and religious experience."

Genetics and The Origin of Species (1997). Francisco Ayala

To calculate the amount of CO$_2$ gas or carbon that was withdrawn by living organisms from the 3.5 BYBP atmosphere to the start of the Cambrian explosion (roughly 541 million years ago) and proceeding to today, we can use two different sets of data.

A) The mass of Earth's atmosphere 3.5 BYBP was similar to that of the present.

At present, the Earth's atmosphere has a mass of 5.15 × 10^{15} metric tons. Assuming that, 3.5 BYBP, the atmosphere had a similar volume (something we don't know for sure) and a similar mass (although its gaseous composition was different, and it probably included a substantial amount of methane CH$_4$), the amount of carbon contained by the primitive atmosphere would have looked like this:

If CO_2 mass contained in the 40-percent CO_2 atmosphere 3.5 BYBP equaled 2×10^{15} tm, then the carbon mass contained in the 40-percent CO_2 atmosphere 3.5 BYBP would be 0.6×10^{15} tm.

About 2.4 billion years later, that is, at the start of the Cambrian explosion, a 0.7-percent CO_2 atmosphere would contain only about 35×10^{12} tm of CO_2, or 9.5×10^{12} tm of elemental carbon.

Today, the CO_2 mass would be one thousandth of the primitive (3.5 BYBP) atmosphere, that is to say, only 2×10^{12} tm of CO_2, or 0.6×10^{12} tm, of carbon.

TABLE 2. CALCULATING THE ATMOSPHERIC CO_2 SUCKED UP BY LIFE-FORMS

Mode of calculation	Type of atmosphere	CO_2 mass in 10^{12} tm	C mass in 10^{12} tm
A	40% CO_2	2,000	600
A	0.7% CO_2	35	9.5
A	Present	2	0.6
B	40% CO_2	3,000	850
B	0.7% CO_2	53	15
B	Present	3	0.8

B) Recalculating back to the past using the present CO_2 mass in our current atmosphere.

The current CO_2 mass in our 0.04-percent CO_2 atmosphere equals 3×10^{12} tm.

Then, for a 0.7-percent CO_2 atmosphere at the time of the Cambrian explosion, the CO_2 mass would have been 53×10^{12} tm of CO_2, or 15×10^{12} tm of carbon content.

Then at the 40-percent CO_2 atmosphere of 3.5 BYBP, the CO_2 content would have been one thousand times the present—3×10^{12} tm of CO_2, or 850×10^{12} tm of carbon.

As can be seen, the differences are pretty dramatic, but this shouldn't surprise us, given that so many assumptions were made in both cases.

But whatever the results, something pretty clear is that somewhere between six and eight hundred trillion tons of carbon were withdrawn from the atmosphere by living organisms in the last 3.5 billion years, an average of 230 metric tons of carbon per year, which is really nonsense.

The maximum amount of 850×10^{12} tons of elemental carbon removed from the atmosphere, according to the data presented in Table 2, is absurdly low and meaningless when compared to the IPPC estimates for the amounts of carbon locked in different sedimentary rocks and formations (see Chapter 2):

TABLE 3: ESTIMATED AMOUNTS OF CARBON LOCKED IN THE UPPER CRUST (*TAKEN FROM IPPC, 4*TH *A.R.*)

CARBON CONTAINED IN	TRILLIONS OF METRIC TONS (10^{12} tm)
Sedimentary carbonates	60,000
Sedimentary kerogens	15,000
Dissolved in the oceans	39.5
Total living mass, including marine	10
Coal (all types)	3.5 *
Inorganic carbon in soils	1.6 **
Live continental organic mass	1
Oil (including bituminous sands and shale)	0.2
Natural gas	0.1 ***
Other	0.2

* The Shunga (Onega Basin, Russia) and Franceville Basin (Gabon) deposits contain the same amount of carbon: 3.5×10^{12} tm. As a comparison, the 2012 estimation of world coal reserves was nine hundred billion tons (0.9×10^{12} tm).
** "Terra preta," carbon not included, estimated about two trillion tons (2×10^{12} tm).
** Methane clathrates (or gas hydrate or methane ice) not included in the above figures are today estimated at about 2.5 trillion tons (2.5×10^{12} tm) of carbon content.

TERRA PRETA DO INDIO

Archeological works compiled mainly by Anna Roosevelt (2013), Balee and Eriksson (2006), and Lehmann (2003) proves that "terra preta" soils are anthropogenic deposits fabricated by ancient indigenous cultures of the Amazon basin about two thousand years ago. The best studied area extends along the Amazon River, between the Marajó Island at the Amazon estuary and the Beni basin in Bolivia, at the foot of the Andean mountain ranges. This type of soil is basically a mineral siliceous and clayish matrix with an extraordinary content of charcoal derived from a controlled system of burning trees (obtaining charcoal in lieu of ashes), food compost (mainly fish spines and bones of animals), pottery shards, and a complex bacterial and fungal microbiota that endow the soil with a high capacity of nutrient retention that translates into an extraordinary fertility.

"Terra preta" was probably developed over at least a quarter of the present Amazonian forest, an area of about six hundred thousand square miles, with soil layers up to ten feet deep and containing an average of 10 percent charcoal. Recent studies are discovering this type of synthetic black soil in Guyana and some locations in the Orinoco basin, while very similar deposits are described in Liberia, Benin, and South Africa. Considering these new findings, a potential total carbon content of "terra preta" soils can be estimated at around 2×10^{12} tons.

According to the opinion of several authors and as summarized in the F. M. Gradstein et al. (2012) book (Chapter 16), the first recorded autotrophs appeared in the ancient seas 3.5 billion years ago. These were cyanobacteria that rapidly started to multiply and fill the oceans' surface, gobbling CO_2 to make up their cellular membranes and cytoplasm, and in the process producing oxygen. But those newly born critters didn't only begin to make carbohydrates, lipids, and protein complexes where carbon was stored as solid organic molecules. Very soon, they amalgamated in extensive colonies that were welded together by thin but extensive biofilms. Some of those biofilms further developed into calcium carbonate, crystalizing nuclei like the current "algal mats." The process resulted in a very common type of finely laminated limestone deposit known by the name of "stromatolite" (*stroma* means mattress in Greek).

Limestone or calcium carbonate is 44 percent CO_2 or 12 percent carbon, so 3.5 billion years ago, cyanobacteria started to gobble CO_2 and fix the gas either as organic matter or as limestone.

According to Gradstein (2012), the De Gray Supergroup in Australia and the Pongola and Witwatersrand Supergroups in South Africa are several kilometers–thick sedimentary sequences that include cyanobacterial calcareous mats and were built three billion years ago. But A. C. Allwood et al. (2007) demonstrated that, many millions of years before that, the Strelley Pool Chert of the Pilbara Craton in Western Australia were silicified thin limestone stromatolites aged 3.43 billion years old, with an average thickness of about ten meters.

Between 3 and 2 BYBP, several organic-rich deposits are known, like the Mt. McRae uranium-rich black shale dated 2.7 billion years or the bituminous shale in the Kaapval Craton dated 2.6 BYBP.

But then, an unprecedented episode took place about 2 BYBP: the Shunga Event—an extraordinary accumulation of organic matter, mainly carbon and fullerenes, so rich that authors like D. Mossman (2003) consider the shungite layers to be a gigantic petrified oil deposit.

The carbon-rich layers found in the Onega Basin (Zaonega Formation) have been divided into very unusual rock types like maksovite, with up to 45 percent carbon content, and anthraxolite with up to 98 percent carbon or bitumolite (Filippov, 2002).

On the average, estimations of the carbon volume in the Russian part of the Onega Basin are calculated as 3 Ttm of elemental carbon, and this is without considering the extensions of the shungite layers into Finland.

PRECAMBRIAN OIL

According to R. Buick et al. (1998), hydrocarbon deposits indicating the genesis of Archean oil were found in different sedimentary rock formations such as in the Pilbara Craton of Australia and in the Witwatersrand Supergroup of the Kaapvaal Craton, which is clear evidence for extensive hydrocarbon generation and migration between 3.5 and 2.5 BYBP.

Later, K. A. R. Ghori et al. (2009) published a synthesis of several Infracambrian petroleum occurrences in several Archean and Proterozoic locations such as the Officer Basin and the McArthur Basin in Australia, where commercial oil is still recovered from sediments dated 1.4 BYBP. The Velkerri Formation (1.5 BYBP) in Northern Australia is considered by Warren (1998) as the organically richest Proterozoic succession in Australia. It is basically made of one thousand feet of laminated organic-rich black shale containing up to 6 percent organic matter.

Organic-rich metamorphosed Proterozoic successions of SE Greenland, the Ukrainian Krivoy Roy Series, and the Canadian Upper Huronian Series also bear oil impregnations in sediments. The Siberian Lena-Tunguska province, the Russian Volga-Ural region, and the Middle Eastern South Oman petroleum fields exemplify the productive potential of the uppermost Neoproterozoic-Cambrian successions.

The authors also stress that the total resource potential of the Lena-Tunguska petroleum province is estimated to be next to two billion barrels of oil and 83 Tcf of natural gas.

More recent is the hydrocarbon-bearing black schist of the Nonesuch Formation, dated about 1 BYBP, and the Chuar Group next to the Colorado River, east of the

Grand Canyon. Both have been classified as potential oil bearing strata.

At about the same epoch, similar extensive, thick layers of uranium-rich black shale (with up to 15 percent carbon content, including fullerenes) and limestone stromatolites of the Franceville Basin were deposited in today's Gabon and are said to contain about five hundred billion tons of elemental carbon. The black shale of the Franceville Formation were first described by D. J. Mossman (2005) and further characterized by F. Gaultier-Lafaye (2006), who compares it with the Shunga Event, while considering it was a worldwide black shale event, related to the stromatolite explosion.

So the question is:

How is it that biological processes were able to synthesize more than $75,000 \times 10^{12}$ tons of carbon, or 300×10^{15} tons of CO_2, into organic molecules along the 3.5 billion years of life on the planet if at the very start there were only 800×10^{12} tons of carbon, or 3×10^{15} tons of carbon dioxide available in the primitive atmosphere?

The only answer to that question is provided in Chapter 8: Geological CO_2 emissions.

As we will see, the planet has been—and still is—degassing for eons, both through volcanic and other hydrothermal activity, mainly transferring CO_2 from deep rocks, the lithosphere, and mantle into the atmosphere. Once in the atmosphere, this volcanic or geological CO_2 was transformed by the vegetation and oceanic life-forms into either organic carbon compounds or limestone.

This transfer of 300×10^{15} tons of CO_2 in the last 3.5 billion years is not a big amount. If we compute it as a yearly rate, it comes out to only eighty-five million tons of CO_2 per year.

This rate of CO_2 withdrawal from the atmosphere is surprisingly small when compared to the present CO_2 drop, which is estimated at twenty thousand billion tons per year (about 250 times smaller).

With a voracious appetite and for billions of years, living organisms have been gulping the atmospheric CO_2 gas to transform it into solid organic or mineral matter (limestone).

This speaks of the current tremendous efficiency of the carbon gobbling or CO_2 gulping power machine that life is. And it also alerts us to the unmatched dangers that such a big drop in CO_2 means to our atmosphere, which is on the very threshold of carbon anoxia.

CHAPTER 6:

THE PLANTS' RESPONSE TO THE CO$_2$ DECREASE

"It appears to us that the current global warming signal lies well within natural limits. In this case, it seems to us difficult to argue that the current global warming signal is the result of human activity."

W. Jackson Davis, Emeritus Professor of Biology, University of California at Santa Cruz, and Peter Taylor, Senior Science and Policy Analyst for the UK organization Ethos and author of Chill: A Reassessment of Global Warming Theory

As discussed in the preceding chapters, there is a great deal of geological evidence that the atmospheric CO$_2$ content fell from the 40 percent of the Proterozoic to today's 0.04 percent.

Such a strong decrease, although spanning over thousands of millions of years, must have had some effect on Earth's biology.

Those effects were particularly dramatic upon plants. Plants are obviously very sensitive to the atmospheric carbon content, given that they depend on CO$_2$ to produce their own food and tissues.

Plants started to conquer the dry-land continents during the Ordovician (475 million years ago). In those days, the planet's atmosphere was still rich in CO$_2$ (about 0.7 percent, which is almost twenty times today's levels), and those first plants had a low number of stomata (sort of "plants' lungs") on their leaves—about five stomata per square millimeter. But a few million years later, in the Carboniferous, plants were "suffocating" in a CO_2-depleted atmosphere that had been halved to only 0.2 percent (five times today's content). The evolutionary tendency toward survival compelled plants to increase the number of stomata per leaf. This number increased twentyfold from five to one hundred per square millimeter. Today, most plants have about the same density of stomata, an intelligent and effective measure for survival when faced with CO_2 anoxia.

It is remarkable that, for a twentyfold drop in CO_2 content in the air, the plants reacted with a twentyfold increase in the number of stomata.

But things grew worse as time elapsed. At the Miocene, about ten million years ago, the CO_2 content of the atmosphere dropped to only 0.1 percent (2.5 times today's levels), and plants were forced to design a new strategy. It was in this Tertiary period when C_4 plants appeared and started colonizing vast regions of the globe.

THE C_4 PLANTS' REVOLUTION

C_4 plants have developed an enhanced biological mechanism of chemical reactions that improve the yield of CO_2 synthesis into organic molecules. C_4 plants can processes the same number of carbon compounds as C_3 plants under lower concentrations of atmospheric CO_2.

Once again, evolution has provided plants with a new metabolic pathway, increasing their efficiency when faced with the progressive depletion of CO_2 in the atmosphere. Nevertheless, we have to mention that some researchers, like Osborne and Beerling (2006), do not agree with the idea that the C_4 metabolic pathway was triggered by declining atmospheric CO_2, although other proposed activating mechanisms don't seem to justify this type of evolutionary response.

Other researchers, like Cerling et al. (1998) and especially Ehleringer et al. (2005), firmly advocate the idea of a new C_4 metabolism as a consequence of the "CO_2 starvation" that began in the Miocene. They claim that the global expansion of the C_4 plants was such an important factor that it even had an effect on the mammalians' diets. In fact, Ehleringer et al. (1997) maintain that C_4-dominated ecosystems didn't expand until atmospheric CO_2 concentrations reached the low levels of the Miocene. And it was precisely at that time when paleocarbonate and fossil data indicate the start of a global expansion of C_4-dominated grasslands.

A remarkable coincidence must be underlined: different experiments aimed at measuring the relation between the biomass yields of different plants under increased CO_2 contents of the surrounding air have found that the C_3 plants' productivity equals that of the C_4 plants when the air contains about 0.07 percent CO_2. Amazingly, that figure is not too far from the assumed 0.1 percent of CO_2 in the Miocene atmosphere.

C_4 plants merely represent 1 percent of all the plant species, but they produce 18 percent of the continental vegetable biomass. Half of all grass species are C_4 plants, and both the largest crops on the planet, corn and sugarcane, are also C_4 plants. Although they first appeared about ten million years ago, C_4 plants went on slowly conquering emerged lands, both barren and productive. Today, prairies, savannas, and crop surfaces are more extensive than forests, and they are likely to increase.

CHAPTER 7:

THE FATE OF PLANTS IN AN ATMOSPHERE OF LESS THAN 0.03 PERCENT CO$_2$

"Historical records show that New York City is at risk of being struck by a hurricane. Four documented strong hurricanes with high storm surges have made landfall in the New York City area since 1693, with the last occurring in 1893."

E. Scileppi and J. P. Donnelly, Geochemistry, Geophysics, Geosystems (2007)

There is ample evidence that high carbon dioxide contents in the air stimulate plant growth. This is because plants have to balance their need for letting carbon dioxide into their cellular photosynthetic factories without letting the water inside their tissues escape as a result of the leaves opening their pores (called stomata). Water is a major limiting factor in plant growth over continental areas, so if there is more CO$_2$ in the air, the stomata on plant leaves do not open as much to get the same amount of carbon dioxide. That way, water can be more easily retained by the plant, enhancing their growth in areas where water is a limiting factor. Lawlor and Mitchell (1991), as well as Gifford (1992) and Poorter (1993), indicate that CO$_2$ studies on crops confirm the results obtained in controlled environments: higher CO$_2$ increases photosynthesis, dry-matter production, and yield, with decreases in stomatal conductance and transpiration, all of which translates to enhanced water-use efficiency in all plants.

A large number of studies deal with the effect of atmospheric CO_2 increase on the growth and physiology of plants. Mayeux (1997) and his colleges, for instance, demonstrated that, without water stress, wheat grows better in high-CO_2 atmospheres, increasing the yield by up to 72 percent. Idso (2000 and 2003) goes much further, measuring yields or production increases of up to 70 percent for C_3 cereals, 28 percent for C_4 cereals, 67 percent for roots and tuber crops, 62 percent for legumes, 51 percent for vegetables, and 33 percent for fruits, each with rising atmospheric CO_2 concentration. Drake and Leadley (1991) revised several studies on the effects of elevated CO_2 on plant growth, all showing that under those conditions there is marked increase of photosynthesis and plant productivity.

Plant growth improves to such a degree that, according to Poorter and Perez-Soba (2001), plants can partially overcome water-stress conditions related to soil salinity.

Curiously enough, Wang et al. (2003) notices that, under an elevated carbon dioxide atmosphere of 600 ppm, the content of antioxidant compounds (flavonols, anthocyanins, and glutathione), as well as vitamin C, increases in both oranges and field-grown strawberries.

The fifteen-year FACE (Free Air CO_2 Experiment) completed at Duke Forest in 2004 is brilliantly summarized in the Ainsworth et al. (2005) paper. Pine trees and plants were subjected to elevated CO_2 atmospheres (without enclosure) of up to 600 ppm that translated in yield increases of up to 8 percent for crop plants and 20 to 25 percent in pine trees (*Pinus taeda* in particular), with a remarkable boost in growth speed, as long as soil fertility and water availability were not affected. These results confirmed previous experiments in closed chambers, with trees being more respondent than herbaceous plants. Leakey (2009) from the University of Illinois at Urbana refers to later experiences on the FACE project more specifically referred to C_4 plants.

On the other hand, a similar experiment as part of the Horsham AGFACE project in Victoria, Australia (Reeves, 2012), found that a CO_2-enriched atmosphere increased crop biomass by 20 percent, while water use was reduced. Some researchers think that under the current atmospheric CO_2 rate of increase, world pine forests would absorb about half of the new gas emissions created as a result of the burning of fuels and deforestation.

SATELLITES PROVE THAT CO_2 INCREASE IS "GREENING" THE WORLD

Rogier de Jong et al. (2011) remarks in his article that data from satellites (1982–2008) provide evidence of changes in land vegetation over almost three decades. The net global tendency is toward an overall "greening," which has been confirmed in previous studies. This net greening was detected in all biomes, although more conspicuously in croplands. Actually, the greening process was advanced by C. D. Keeling in 1996 when discussing the amplitude of the seasonal increase of CO_2, with increased assimilation of CO_2 by land plants (mass vegetation increase).

Later, Xu et al. in a 2013 paper confirmed that the greening of the Earth has now been going on for thirty years. Between 1982 and 2011, 20.5 percent of the world's vegetated area got greener, while just 3 percent grew browner; the rest showed no change. To have a perspective of the amazing significance of these figures, one has to think that 20.5 percent of the world's vegetated area represents 3.5 million square miles, nearly the total area of the United States. A thorough study of the available data implies that, in 50 percent of the vegetated areas, the greening is an effect of general warming and more rainfall, while in the other half, these two variables didn't change during the period, making it is highly probable that **the greening effect was caused by carbon dioxide fertilization**. This is in agreement with many experiments showing that plants improve productivity and leaf extension under increased CO_2 levels.

The greening effect means that over the past fifty years, global carbon uptake has doubled from two billion tons in 1960 to 5.0 billion tons in 2010. One has to consider that this trend occurred in spite of the occurrence of several catastrophic events such as wildfires, tsunamis, and more continuous irreversible processes such as progressive urbanization and deforestation due to human population growth.

It is pretty clear that the atmospheric CO_2 increase seems to improve vegetation both in extension and productivity rather than being a noxious poison to the green world.

On the other hand, Wang et al. (2014) have measured a twofold increase of the CO_2-reducing capacity of the world's vegetation in the last fifty years and signal that this fact is in conflict with the current climate models predicting global climate change.

Since C. D. Keeling began collecting data on the atmospheric concentration of carbon dioxide at the Mauna Loa monitoring station in Hawaii back in 1958, a continuous regular variation was detected and called "seasonal cycle," since CO_2 emissions were higher at the end of the northern hemisphere's summer and lower in winter. Kohlmeier (1987) and Thoning (1989) were probably the first to detect a change in the amplitude of the cycle, which since then has been referred to as the seasonal cycle amplitude (SCA). Surprisingly, it was found that SCA was increasing from fluctuations of less than 5 ppm back in 1958 to about 7 ppm thirty years later. In the following years, new data were obtained from other monitoring stations located at higher and lower latitudes than Mauna Loa, as well as measurements collected by airplane detectors following different routes. It was then found that SCA was several parts per million wider than the original Mauna Loa records and that, according to the data presented by Keeling in his 1996 paper, it became pretty clear that SCA regularly increased from the equator to higher latitudes in the northern hemisphere while contrasting to a very narrow SCA of only two or three parts per million south of the equator.

In 2011, for instance, SCA varied from 18 ppm CO_2 at 80° north to only 6 ppm at 20° north, while it drops to 2–3 ppm at the equator and about 1–2 ppm in all latitudes of the southern hemisphere.

This time and latitude variation of the SCA is explained by different authors as the result of three main effects:

—CO_2 fertilization: plants increase the efficiency in CO_2 absorption, something that translates into a better organic yield or productivity.

—Green revolution: increase of the crops' mass as a result of the use of high-yield breeds, fertilizers, pest management, and irrigation.

—Expansion of the vegetal cover due to high latitude warming that changes tundra into taiga (poleward migration of ecosystems) or savanna cover winning over deserts. Moreover, Barichivich (2013) reports that compared to thirty years ago, the Arctic growing season is six days longer in North America and thirteen days longer in Eurasia, a fact that translates in the progressive expansion of the taiga forest at the expense of the tundra.

However, and following MacDonald et al. (2008), conifers have not yet recolonized many areas where trees were present during the Medieval Warm period (ca AD 800–1300) or the Holocene Thermal Maximum (HTM; ca 10 000–3000 years ago).

Of course, these factors widely compensate for the well-known overall reduction of the vegetation cover implied by the expansion of residential areas of cities, the industrial growth, wildfires, mangrove forests degradation, and soil salinization.

Another factor that is worth considering is the retarding effect of CO_2 dissolving in the Arctic waters after the summer thaw. According to Bates (2006), the ice cover blocks the gas exchange between the Arctic Ocean and the atmosphere, but once this frozen barrier melts in the summer, millions of tons of atmospheric CO_2 are absorbed by the sea.

IS THE SAHARA DESERT GREENING?

After analyzing satellite data, Seaquist (2006) and his colleagues report an increase of net primary production

(NPP) of carbon content in a vegetation band beginning approximately at 17° north and extending from Senegal to Southern Sudan for the period 1982 to 1999. This increase was equivalent to fifty-one million tons of carbon capture per year and was attributed to both atmospheric CO_2 and rainfall increase.

These figures confirm previous observations by Eklundh and Olsson (2003) and Olsson, Eklundh, and Ardo (2005). These researchers have noticed a consistent trend of increasing vegetation greenness in much of the Sahel (the southern fringe of the Sahara), a fact explained not only by an increase in rainfall in the two last decades, but also by the reduction in land use and the drop in overgrazing and deforestation.

A somewhat similar study was completed by a total of thirty-three researchers (Lewis et al. 2009) across a larger time lapse (1968–2007), measuring a moist, closed-canopy African forest and finding a carbon sink of 340 million tons per year. Similar studies completed over the Amazon and other Asian and American tropical forests resulted in an estimated of carbon sink of about 1.3 billion tons per year of carbon during the last decades.

Scheiter and Higgins (2009) use an adaptive dynamic global vegetation model (aDGVM) to suggest that grasslands will spread into the Sahara with an almost 6 percent decrease of the desert area by 2100. The model also predicts that about 45 percent of the present savannas will turn into deciduous forests, with a roughly 200-percent total increase in biomass.

According to Donovan (1991), more efficient use of water by plants growing in richer CO_2 environments will result in the reduction of their stomata openings, which means more growth for the same water availability. This was later confirmed by Trenberth et al. (2014), who calculated that water efficiency grows six times faster than the CO_2 enrichment. At the same time, more growth will buffer CO_2 increases, which is bad news for doomsters like Pearson et al. (2013), claiming that less tundra means less albedo and further warming acceleration.

From all the above analyzed studies, it is pretty clear that the future CO_2 air enrichment and its associated increase in water use efficiency in plants translates to an overall greening effect of the Sahara desert, an effect that is already showing in the South Saharan marginal band at approximately the 17° north parallel.

On the contrary, there are scant studies on the subject of how plants are affected by a CO_2 decrease.

There is a broad consensus that plants in general (trees more than grasses, and C_3 plants more than C_4 plants) start to be seriously affected when CO_2 concentration falls below 200 ppm. The crucial threshold is considered 160 ppm, below which RuBisCo and other enzymes (rubisco is the enzyme involved at the start of carbon fixation the metabolic process in plants that convert carbon dioxide into glucose and other organic molecules) stop working and photosynthesis is halted.

Studies by Allen et al. (1991), Dippery et al. (1995), and Polley et al. (1992) show that, on the average, the growth of C_3 plants is reduced by approximately 60 percent (in some species up to about 90 percent) in the 180–220 ppm CO_2 concentration range, when compared to present conditions. Data on the test done with samples of emmer wheat (*Triticum dicoccum*) are particularly worrisome, showing decreases in growth between 8 and 53 percent, depending on the average temperature. Plants' reproductive capacity, although largely unknown, seems to be greatly compromised. Moreover, under low CO_2 conditions, stress factors such as drought, freezing cold, pests, or low nutrient availability may have more marked effects on plant growth and physiology. In a following paper Polley et al. (1993) presents data indicating that this increase in CO2 from the Glacial Maximum, about 18,000 years ago (about 200 ppm) to the present levels, has enhanced biospheric carbon fixation and altered species abundances by increasing the water-use efficiency of biomass production of C3 plants, the bulk of the Earth's vegetation. Leaf water-use efficiency and above-ground biomass/plant of C3 species increased linearly and nearly proportionally with increasing CO2 concentrations.

Beerling (2012) concludes that NPP (net primary production/year) and biomass of trees falls to half if atmospheric CO_2 content is halved from 400 to 200 ppm and drops to near zero at 100 ppm. A similar drop happens to C_4 grasses, while C_3 grasses are least affected.

All plants (except C_3 grasses) are visibly affected when CO_2 drops from 400 to 300 ppm, showing about 10 percent decrease in NPP and biomass in trees, a similar decrease in NPP in the case of C_4 grasses, and only a 5 percent decrease in biomass.

In earlier studies by Dippery et al. (1995) found that there was almost zero growth in total biomass in the case of C_3 plants at contents of 150 ppm in controlled growth chambers, while C_4 plants (*Amaranthus retroflexus*) were not affected, even at low contents of 100 ppm CO_2.

Gerhart and Ward (2010) provide a complete up-date on the subject and show a number of graphs and figures clearly representing the fall in both growth and biomass when different plants are grown at close to 200 ppm CO_2 atmosphere.

As a conclusion, we have to emphasize that the majority of plants will be seriously affected if the CO_2 content in our atmosphere drops below 0.02 percent (200 ppm), while C_4 plants and probably most of the grasses will stay unaffected. In any event, it is highly probable that some reductions in crop yield and reproductive functions could start affecting plants if CO_2 drops below 0.03 percent (300 ppm).

Sage (1995) considers that CO_2 levels below 200 ppm may be too low to support the level of productivity required for the successful establishment of agriculture. He points out a very convincing argument, stating that high biomass productivity (above 300 ppm) is necessary for C_3 plants to compete with weedy C_4s.

CHAPTER 8:

NATURAL GEOLOGICAL CO$_2$ EMISSIONS (NONBIOGENIC)

The new religion of global warming is a great story, and a phenomenal best-seller. It contains a grain of truth and a mountain of nonsense. And that nonsense could be very damaging indeed. We appear to have entered a new age of unreason, which threatens to be as economically harmful as it is profoundly disquieting. It is from this, above all, that we really do need to save the planet.

Nigel Lawson (2008). An Appeal to Reason: A Cool Look at Global Warming

Given the scant number of papers on this subject, the volume of natural CO$_2$ emissions generated by volcanic and related activities (dormant volcanoes, hydrothermal vents, gas-rich thermal sources, active faulted terrains, areas of frequent earthquakes and associated phenomena, etc.) is probably one of the least-studied subjects regarding the cycle or balance of the atmospheric CO$_2$.

Nevertheless, degassing processes on the Earth's crust have been identified and described in thousands of localities in the world. Some of those areas are famous touristic attractions like the Yellowstone caldera or the Ten Thousand Smokes Valley in Alaska. Other less famous localities where gas is seeping through at a rate of several thousand tons per day are scattered throughout the world, including the Furnas volcanic lake (Azores Islands, Portugal), the Mammoth Mountain,

Horseshoe Lake, Sierra Nevada in California, or the Laacher See, a maar (volcanic) lake in Germany.

Rarely, CO_2 emissions from volcanic slopes or lakes can literally "burn" forests and asphyxiate animals or even humans, as recorded during the sad incidents of CO_2 releases from Lake Nyos and Lake Monoun—both located on the Cameroon Volcanic Line that extends for about one thousand miles in Western Africa—that killed nearly two thousand people in 1984 and 1986. Lake Kivu in Ruanda is also a deadly candidate with continuous bubbling of CO_2 and methane. Similar deadly accidents occurred around lakes in the Dieng volcanic complex in Java, killing a total of 150 people in 1979 and 1992.

Emeritus Professor Ian R. Plimer (2009) from the University of Melbourne has argued for many years that volcanic eruptions release more carbon dioxide and that the influence of the gases from these volcanoes on the Earth's climate is drastically underrepresented in the climate models.

In 2000, G. Chiodini, a researcher working at the Italian Istituto Nazionale di Geofisica e Vulcanologia, presented a very interesting paper in the *Journal of Geophysical Research*. For many years, the author and his fellow collaborators measured the amount of CO_2 gases that were released from volcanoes in Italy and compared the data with similar figures obtained by other researchers worldwide.

According to Chiodini and his fellow collaborators, for instance, the Etna (Italy) volcano ejects some twenty-five million tons of CO_2 per year through its crater, plus another five million metric tons through its flanks, an impressive amount when compared to the Kilauea (Hawaii) crater that spews only seven million tons of CO_2 a year.

When comparing this data with the overall world CO_2 emissions of either volcanic or nonvolcanic origin as published by Kerrick (2001), Mörner, and Etiope (2002), and later by Hards (2005), all of which putting the figure somewhere between three and six hundred million tons a year, we cannot help feeling surprised. The Etna by itself degasses a yearly mass of CO_2 equivalent to 5–10 percent of the world's total!

Somewhere, something must be wrong.

In its official internet page (www.usgs.gov) the US Geological Survey endorses an average of 130 million tons a year, that is only about four times de Etna emissions while in the same page, the USGS reports that every other day there are a minimum of twenty active volcanoes emitting material and gases in the world, not counting submarine emissions, of course. According to data published by the Smithsonian and the USGS, there were 550 documented eruptions during the last decade. No one presents figures on the estimated or measured CO_2 emissions, but we know, for instance, that according to the P. Allard 2011 paper, the April 2010 eruption of Eyjafjallajokull in Iceland produced an average of one hundred and fifty thousand tons of carbon dioxide a day, a rate of about fifty five million metric tons per year, about the half of the USGS world average.

But Chiodini's paper has more to reveal.

According to his measurements, the Italian fumaroles fields (Italy is an important producer of geothermal energy) deliver half a million tons of CO_2 to the atmosphere every year, while in nonvolcanic areas such as the central Apennines, CO_2 emanations reach between four and thirteen tons of CO_2 per year over an area of eight thousand square miles, figures that have been confirmed by different studies published by different researchers.

So, this is Dr. Chiodini's conclusion:

All geological or tectonic CO_2 sources (volcanic and related activities) considered, the Italian territory is degassing at a minimum total average rate of fifty million tons per year over its continental extension (the Etna by itself represents 60 percent of that figure).

One could assume that Italy is an anomalous area of the earth's crust, with an exceptional number of both active and dormant volcanoes (remember Pompeii), although it is not too different from other "volcanic-bond" areas like Japan, Indonesia, Chile, Iceland, the African Rift Valley, or Mexico. For the sake of a high confidence level, we shall only consider 10 percent of the Italian discharges to estimate the world's total geological CO_2 emissions.

The area of Italy is roughly 116,350 square miles, and the worlds' continental surface is 51,200,000 square miles (excluding Greenland and Antarctica, although the latter has several active volcanoes piercing the ice sheet cover). With these numbers, the total CO_2 geological flux would come to about two billion tons of CO_2 a year.

We shall also assume that the oceanic geological CO_2 releases by degassing is similar to the continental one, and considering that the oceans extend for 139 million square miles, delivery of CO_2 would be about five billion tm/year, and the grand planetary total would be **seven billion tons of CO_2 emitted per year, a volume that represents about a quarter of the anthropogenic emissions.**

These may seem exaggerated figures, compared to the three to six hundred million tons quoted in the above lines (about ten times more), but one must take into account the facts presented by the many experts such as oceanographers Hillier and Watts (2007), who surveyed 201,055 submarine volcanoes and estimate that the Earth's oceanic floor must be dotted by some 3.5 million volcanoes, most of which are either actively or passively seeping CO_2.

Seven billion tons of CO_2 a year means that crustal degassing is increasing the CO_2 content of the planet's atmosphere at about 1.5 ppm/year (see Table 4).

This is 1.5 ppm more of CO_2 per year.

Keep these figures in mind, because they are the key to understanding what's going on.

CHAPTER 9:

CO$_2$ DEPLETION RATES

"What does it mean that the temperature has gone up 0.8 degrees? Probably nothing."

"Is climate change pseudoscience? If I'm going to answer the question, the answer is: absolutely."

1973 Nobel Prize winner Ivar Giaever

There seems to be a lot of confusion on the historical rates of atmospheric CO$_2$ depletion.

If we go back to Figure 1, we observe that atmospheric CO$_2$ content dropped from the 40 percent that existed 3.5 BYBP to only 0.7 percent (7,000 ppm) at the Cambrian life explosion (541 MYBP). This means that in 2.95 billion years, the atmospheric CO$_2$ content dropped at a rate of 0.0133 percent every million years, or 133 ppm per million years.

But if we consider Figure 2, we find that the drop has been less dramatic in the last 550 million years: only about 12 ppm per million years, or ten times less than in the Precambrian days.

According to these figures, the yearly CO$_2$ depletion of our atmosphere is insignificant: less than 0.0001 ppm/year.

CAMBRIAN EXPLOSION?

Although most geologists consider that life in the planet changed abruptly at the beginning of the "Cambrian explosion" with the advent of many new taxa never found in older geological layers (of the thirty-five recognized phyla, only three show evidence of being Precambrian), it is necessary to remember that new evidence of complex life-forms is being found increasingly all around the planet. *Namapoikia rietoogensis* is one example of how complex life was just little before the dawn of the Cambrian, 549 MYBP (about eight million years before the Cambrian). Wood et al. (2002) describe this new metazoan found in the Omkyk Member of the Nama Group in Namibia. This strange marine animal has a three-foot diameter and a stunning biomineralized skeleton. *Namapoikia* lived in the walls of fissures open in microbial reef mats and is a fair example of a complex life-form quite different to unicellular or microscopic organisms.

On the other hand, we have completely different figures that result from the last twenty years of a massive number of studies that were dedicated to calculating the amount of CO_2 that is emitted in the atmosphere by different biological (nonanthropogenic) sources or, better said, to calculate the balance between the CO_2 coming out of living systems into the atmosphere and the flux absorbed by the same. Today, most experts consider that apart from anthropogenic discharges, the earth's surface (both continental and oceanic areas) releases some seven billion tons of CO_2 a year, an amount that is counterbalanced by the biological absorption of 720 billion tons, that is to say that under current normal conditions, the earth's biological mass *sinks twenty billion tons of CO_2 a year.*
In other words, life reduces the CO_2 content of the atmosphere by an average of 4 ppm/year (according to Table 4).

TABLE 4. MASS OF CO_2 IN THE ATMOSPHERE IN RELATION TO ITS PROPORTION IN THE AIR (IN PPM)

Ppm of CO_2 in atmosphere	Mass of CO_2 (in billion tons or Gt)
400	2,000
350	1,750
300	1,500
250	1,250
200	1,000
150	750
100	500
50	250

This is quite far from the less than 0.0001 ppm/year estimated by the historical decrease along the last 3.5 BYBP. Yet no one has explained why.

On the other side, as we have seen at the end of Chapter 4, the rate of biological CO_2 absorption has increased two hundred times when compared to past geological rates. This is an important fact to take into account.

The rate of extraction or sinking of atmospheric CO_2 by the biological complex (plants and marine organisms) has intensively accelerated in the last million years when compared to the past.

Although the figures are difficult to reconcile, one thing is for certain: the Earth's biology is and has been losing CO_2 from its atmosphere for the last 3.5 billion years. And today, that rate is a substantial amount: 4 ppm/year.

But we cannot forget that the Earth's crust is degassing at a rate of 1.5 ppm/year (see Chapter 8), so that the current balance is an atmospheric loss of **2.5 ppm/year** of CO_2.

This is a worrisome figure, since it means that in a century—provided we stop or dramatically reduce anthropogenic CO_2 emissions—the carbon dioxide content of our atmosphere will decline to about 150 ppm.

This is a terribly low level, since, as was shown in Chapter 7, the majority of plants will not be able to survive.

But it happened before.

CHAPTER 10:

IT HAPPENED BEFORE, ABOUT TWELVE THOUSAND YEARS AGO

"Have we delayed a glaciation? The evidence seems clear: human activities linked to farming had taken control of the natural trends of the major greenhouse gases thousands of years ago, forcing their concentration to rise when nature would have driven them lower."

William F. Ruddiman, Plow, Plagues, and Petroleum (2005)

The fact that the voracious gorging of CO_2 by the vegetable mass of the planet has put the biosphere's own existence in jeopardy has been recorded in several instances in the last eight hundred thousand years, as evidenced by the ice records of both the Arctic and Antarctic ice caps. In at least four occasions, the CO_2 content of the atmosphere fell below the 200 ppm deadly threshold that puts plant life at extinction's edge. Much before that, as soon as the CO_2 content fell below 300 ppm and temperatures dropped a couple of degrees, plants started suffering an intensive stress that generated changes in their metabolism, reproduction hitches, and growth anomalies, all accelerating the process.

Fortunately, the combination of the plants' anoxia and the death of substantial vegetable masses triggered under an atmosphere of under 200 ppm of CO_2, which erased most of the vegetation cover and reduced the plummeting carbon dioxide levels. This offset or curbed the atmospheric CO_2 depletion process, bringing the CO_2 absorption rate of 4 ppm/year to what was probably well below 1 ppm/year (cyanobacteria being the major consumers of CO_2 due to their incredible survival rates, even under freezing conditions).

At this stage, the degassing rate of the crust through volcanic and tectonic emissions (1.5 ppm/year) reversed the balance, and slowly the normal carbon dioxide stock replenished and brought the CO_2 contents back to the average of 300 ppm, under which normal warmer temperatures returned and there was enough CO_2 in the atmosphere to bring the vegetation back to its former lush state.

And then the cycle repeated again—at least eight times in the last eight hundred thousand years.

In the old pre-Quaternary days, the atmospheric CO_2 contents were well above 400–500 ppm. There were no glacial cycles, or at least none triggered by the drop in CO_2 caused by the expansion of vegetation.

But today, we are hovering very near the brink of plants' annihilation as a result of a lack of CO_2. Any shift away from this delicate equilibrium could result in disaster.

Our own life and the biology of the planet hang by a very thin string of only 200 ppm, the difference between the plants' lavish life and their exhaustion.

According to the available ice core records, in several instances in the last eight hundred thousand years, the atmospheric CO_2 levels were oscillating dangerously between 200 and 182 ppm (cold intervals), which is distinctive of several cycles of glaciations, with average world temperatures dropping down to eight degrees centigrade below today's standard and thus making uninhabitable a great fraction of the continental lands (Tripati et al. 2009).

But the last cooling cycle took place quite recently: about twelve thousand years ago.

THE YOUNGER DRYAS

Stomatal data presented by Wagner et al. (2004), Finsinger et al. (2009), McElwain et al. (2002), and other researchers show that in the last fourteen thousand years, CO_2 levels fluctuated between 340 and

260 ppm, but a dangerous freezing event took place about 12,000 YBP, an event known as the Younger Dryas, a time when CO_2 levels dropped to a frightening 180 ppm.

The Younger Dryas stadial is also known as the "Big Freeze," the result of a rapid collapse of northern hemisphere temperatures that lasted between 12,900 and 11,500 YBP and was caused by an unknown but broadly disputed series of events that go from thermohaline current interruptions to solar and space-related events.

Three astonishing features characterize this recent event:

—Its short duration, when compared to the longer interglacial warm periods.

—The sudden and dramatic drop in temperatures (some researchers believe that average temperatures fell somewhere between five and fifteen degrees centigrade in just one decade), which demands novel and exceptional explanations (abrupt climate change).

—There are many indications that the freezing was limited to the northern hemisphere. Kaplan (2010) found that signs of a cooling spell in the southern hemisphere are either absent or not exactly synchronous, and when present, they indicate a smaller degree of cooling that never reached the northern hemisphere's intensity.

In addition to data obtained from the study of ice cores (mostly in Greenland), the Younger Dryas cooling is basically summarized by the substitution of forest (taiga) areas by tundra vegetation (shrubs, lichens, and peatlands), glaciers advancing in mountain areas, and drought in the lower latitude deserts that show up as loess deposits and/or dust-rich layers in ice cores, ocean cores, and lake sediments.

According to the synthesis maps of paleovegetation drawn by J. M. Adams and his collaborators (1998), during the Younger Dryas, most of the present Canadian territory was covered by ice, except for the area today represented by the Winnipeg-Saskatchewan provinces, where there was a mixture of forest and tundra. South of the Canadian border, the northern US vegetation was either "semidesert" or "mid-taiga," with grasslands only showing in a belt extending southward from North Dakota and Montana. Meanwhile in Europe, Scandinavia was totally covered by ice, Northern Russia was a "polar desert," and from the approximate latitudes of Southern Russia to Northern France, there was "tundra-steppe" (a grass-and-shrubs cold steppe different from today's tundra), and south of it (Northern Mediterranean-Rumania-Ukraine), there existed a "dry steppe."

As can be gathered from these maps, a generally cold and dry situation characterized most of the northern hemisphere north of 40° north, a rather unfriendly situation for big grazers. Therefore, it seems possible that such a rapid change in climate would have been followed by a brutal change in vegetation that consequentially triggered a dramatic famine, which likely seriously affected the big grazers given their need for large amounts of grasses rich in nutrients for their daily sustenance. Failing this, starvation or a deficient immune system made them victims of a cooling spell, driving them into decimation or extinction.

Coinciding with the Younger Dryas event, the northern hemisphere witnessed an incredible mass extinction of large animals and, more specifically, very large-bodied mammals such as mammoths, giant ground sloths, woolly rhinoceros, camels, American horses, and many other species. Most were completely wiped out, while others, like the mammoths, thoroughly decimated. But the most remarkable point is not the extinction event in itself, whatever the importance of its biological meaning. The incredible fact is that most of the large animals—although not extinct—died by the thousands, and in several northern high latitudes, many were literally found "frozen to death."

Dozens of mammoth corpses were found still imprisoned in the permafrost ice, almost untouched, their woolly fur coats perfectly retaining their vivid reddish colors—the skin, the thick protective layer of fat, the flesh and muscles, and even the most internal organs remained in a perfect state. In his book of frozen animal mummies found in the northern permafrost, D. R. Guthrie (1990) describes the findings of many different animals, each with its organs and stomach contents perfectly preserved, a fact that can only be explained by very rapid cooling events—a matter of mere hours—so that thawed corpses would keep their proteins and fats "fresh" for thousands of years.

Several hypotheses have been proposed by different authors to explain such massive extinctions, including excessive human hunting or the more widely accepted theory of a rapid climate shift.

Lately, Ross MacPhee (2013), a curator of mammalogy at the American Museum of Natural History in New York, has proposed a new plot: a lethal disease, brought over by humans when they started their expansion and colonization over the northern lands. This hyperdisease hypothesis is based on similar events that occurred in other areas of the world a few thousand years later. There is a great deal of agreement and rather solid evidence that in isolated places like Australia, Madagascar, and New Guinea, megafaunal extinctions followed the arrival of humans, together with their own domestic animals, carrying bacteria, viruses, and other pathogenic microorganisms against which local animals' immunological arsenals were defenseless.

The disputable point in MacPhee's hypothesis is that all known examples of lethal disease-related extinctions involve just one or a minimum number of species, something that is hard to match up with the fact that, in the Americas, some 130 species of animals dispersed throughout different climatic environments disappeared in about a millennium. Another point that remains unresolved by this theory is the circumstance that similar massive deaths and extinctions were registered at the same time in Europe and Asia (especially in Siberia) during the Younger Dryas stadial in areas of long-dated human occupation. On the other side, compared to other hypothesis, the disease theory allows for the survival of other big mammals like moose, elk, or bison, probably because of their different genotype. Mammoths, in fact, survived many thousands of years after the Younger Dryas. The last specimens were found in Russia's Wrangler Island and dated 4,000 YBP.

Meanwhile, MacPhee and his colleges are busy studying extinct animal remains, looking for foreign DNA that could be related to bacterial or viral pathogens to confirm their hypothesis.

There is also the meteoritic impact hypotheses that was first advanced by Firestone (2007), by which a series of impacts built the Great Lakes of North America and at the same time triggered the collapse of massive glacial ice caps that fused together, rapidly changing the "heat conveyor belt" (thermohaline circulation) of the Gulf Stream and producing the temperature collapse. This theory is not accepted by the expert majority, since it doesn't explain why a Gulf Stream collapse would affect temperatures in the southern hemisphere, although this area of the planet did suffer from a milder cooling. Moreover, the present heating effects of the Gulf Stream do not affect the Siberian landmass temperatures, and this same relationship would likely have been valid in the past.

But theories apart, the most stunning characteristic of the Younger Dryas was the sudden and brutal drop in average temperatures (estimated between 7° and 12° centigrade) and the persistence of polar type weather during the span of 1,400 years. This is a fact capable by itself of causing widespread extinctions and the decimation of both animals and human beings over most of the higher latitudes in the world.

Based on MacPhee's hypothesis, we can attempt a new one that combines the lethal disease idea with exceptional cold climatic conditions.

Compared to previous glaciation events, the Dryas was a super-cooling event, as is evidenced by the dramatically large extinctions that spared animals and humans in the previous eight glacial events in the last eight hundred thousand years.

The feedback effect of dropping atmospheric CO_2 and temperatures brought vegetation to a halt, eliciting death by either starvation or hunger to most big mammals, or at least causing such a high grade of physical weakness due to stress and lack of nutrients that, in many species, their immune systems became ineffective and fell prey to viral or bacterial pathogens.

Why did the Younger Dryas cooling stop? Why did this rapid cooling last only 1,400 years compared to an average of thirty thousand years for the previous recent (Pleistocene) glaciations? Several authors think it could be the result of early human activity.

CHAPTER 11:

WE ARE FACING
A THREATENING SITUATION

"Stories about climate change teach us that we should be more alert to these climate risks, that we should seek to reduce the number of people who are vulnerable to them, and that we should seek new ways to protect those who remain exposed to these risks."

Professor Mike Hulme, "The Five Lessons of Climate Change: A Personal Statement" (2008)

As shown in previous chapters, it seems undeniable that the decrease and fluctuations in the planet's CO_2 levels are *life*-related, itself probably affected by exceptional catastrophic events like the Chicxulub extinction. We are making slow progress into understanding how life influences the physical constraints of our planet. Very recently, we learned that coral reefs are able to control their local atmospheric conditions by emitting chemicals into the atmosphere that act like cloud-forming seeds. In the future, we will probably know more about airborne bacteria and their cloud-forming impact.

Is Earth's climate just the result of physics and thermodynamics, or should life be introduced as a new term in the equation?

The present threatening situation is a consequence of the fact that, several times in the last eight hundred thousand years, we have reached such low atmospheric CO_2 levels that, on top of reducing temperatures by several degrees, resulting in the generation of ice caps and glaciers, such low levels very probably affected plants' life or survival—and undoubtedly their nutrient contents and reproduction.

These cycles are explained here as a sequence of extreme vegetation-related sink of CO_2, that generates a drop in atmospheric CO_2 that in turn translates into average temperature decrease, causing the annihilation of plants due to combined CO_2 anoxia and extreme cold. At this stage, a glacial event follows, a situation that is very slowly amended by the geological CO_2 emissions that improve the atmospheric CO_2 levels and warm the planet out of its glacial period. Then the cycle repeats again.

If we look at Figure 3, we can see a pretty clear cycle of events that were recorded in the combined ice cores of Vostok and Epic that show the atmospheric variation of CO_2 in the last eight hundred thousand years.

FIGURE 3. LONGEST ICE CORE DATA FROM ANTARCTIC GLACIERS *Source: Carbon Dioxide Information Analysis Center (CDIAC), US Department of Energy, Office of Science, Oak Ridge National Laboratory.*

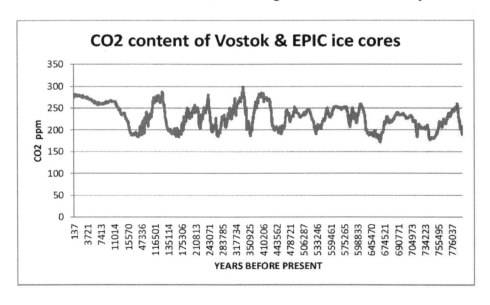

A more detailed examination of this five-stage cyclic process follows:

STAGE 1: WARMTH
We start the cycle at a moment when the climate is warm, the CO_2 content of the atmosphere is about 350 ppm, and vegetation is fully growing and expanding. The taiga occupies most of the tundra extension. The Arctic sea is free of ice, with cyanobacteria activity fully developing. The carbon absorption triggered by this situation is at maximum. As the Arctic Sea and tundra-taiga show no ice cover—the albedo effect is nil.

EARLY STAGE 2: SLIGHT COOLING
Under the strong carbon absorption triggered by the extensive and intensive photosynthesizing activity at Stage 1, the amount of atmospheric CO_2 starts to decrease and drops below 300 ppm—at first without affecting the amount of carbon absorption. Average temperatures begin to drop.

LATE STAGE 2: RAPID COOLING
Atmospheric CO_2 is now around 200 ppm, and temperatures are falling rapidly. Vegetation cover is affected by both lower temperatures and lower CO_2 content in the atmosphere. The tundra extends at the expense of a diminishing taiga. The Artic Sea begins to freeze, and albedo is increasing.

STAGE 3: GLACIAL
Vegetation is disappearing due to CO_2 anoxia (180 to 150 ppm), ice and snow cover great boreal extensions, and the albedo effect is at maximum. Little by little, geological CO_2 increases the atmospheric CO_2 content.

STAGE 4: EARLY WARMING
Accumulation of geological CO_2 in the atmosphere brings its content over 200 ppm. Slowly, the Earth warms, and vegetation starts to increase.

STAGE 5: INCREASED WARMING

Geological CO_2 and increasing photosynthesis brings atmospheric CO_2 content to around 250 ppm. Temperatures are slowly increasing, and vegetation growth is favored by a warmer climate and more CO_2 in the atmosphere. The Arctic Sea starts to lose its ice cover, and the taiga is starting to occupy the tundra spaces.

STAGE 1: WARMTH

The cycle repeats.

TABLE 5. POSSIBLE EXPLANATION FOR THE GLACIAL-INTERGLACIAL CYCLES

	WARM	EARLY COOLING	LATE COOLING	GLACIAL	EARLY WARMING	INCREASED WARMING
Vegetation cover	Extreme	High but decreasing	Strongly diminishing	Near extinction	Slowly expanding	Rapidly expanding
Phytoplankton	Utmost	Decreasing	Almost nil	Nil	Almost nil	Increasing
Atmospheric CO_2	Highest 350 ppm	Drops to 250 ppm	Drops to 200 ppm	Less than 180 ppm	More than 200 ppm	More than 250 ppm
CO_2 sink	Highest	Diminishing	Almost nil	Nil	Almost nil	Increasing
Boreal albedo	Nil	Increasing	Extensive	Maximum	Extensive	Diminishing
CO2 sequesting by carbonate organisms	Highest	Decreasing	Almost nil	Nil	Increasing	Rapid increase

This dangerous situation of atmospheric CO_2 concentrations getting so close to the limit where most plants can be affected in both yield and growth, including the extinction of the more sensitive species, was providentially stopped about two centuries ago when the industrial revolution initiated the burning of significant amounts of fossil fuels, resulting in great amounts of carbon dioxide being emitted into the atmosphere.

On the contrary, and as has happened in the past million years, an anthropogenic increase of CO_2 will accelerate plant metabolism and nutrients synthesis (more carbohydrates, lipids, proteins, etc.), triggering an enhancement in vegetation mass that in itself will buffer some of the CO_2 increase. Soil microorganism activity will also increase, resulting in stronger weathering of silicates, which will also help in buffering some of the carbon dioxide increase by the neoformation of carbonate (CO_3) minerals and increasing cationic absorption of clay minerals. Ocean-wise, it will increase carbon sequestration, which will translate in future coal-gas-oil deposits in anoxic basins. On the other hand, it will promote shell-forming organisms and stimulate coral and other calcareous-building organisms, which as a result will also partially buffer the waters' CO_2 increase by blocking the carbon as stable limestone (CO_3Ca-Mg) deposits.

By undertaking the industrial revolution, humankind rerouted the natural course of CO_2 depletion, reversing the dangerous natural trend initiated some 3.5 billion years ago.

CONCLUSIONS

"Global warming has become the new religion."

1973 Nobel Prize winner Ivar Giaever

Life is the most fantastic phenomenon that is taking place in our planet. For many years, many people have been looking for exoplanets, but still, although candidates number in the hundreds, not a similar life-containing planet has yet been found.

Life is incredibly fantastic and exceptional. It is the result of an extraordinary convergence of exceptional factors. One wonders if such a special situation is bound to be repeated somewhere else in the universe.

Our planet has been home to life for at least 3.5 billion years, of which the last five hundred million were sort of miracle, a landscape of utmost beauty.

Not only beautiful, but also extremely complex, with new creatures still being discovered after centuries of scientific search and classification. It is difficult for a human mind to conceive of a new creature that is not already roaming around somewhere or had been wandering over our planet in the geological past.

But miracles have a price. Everything in nature is consequential.

Life was a consequence of many things, but among them is one crucial component: a primitive atmosphere rich in carbon dioxide. Life started and developed by absorbing the abundant CO_2 content of that primitive atmosphere. It then grew in a bountiful organic complex that filled all the available ecological niches on the planet, from the highest mountain summits to the deepest dark sea trenches. From the freezing polar temperatures to the sun's scorched deserts and hot humid jungles. And beyond, deep below the surface, at more than a thousand meters depth, in newly opened mine galleries, life-forms were found. There is life even under the radiation-flooded environment of a nuclear reactor. There are bacteria in the air, up to thousands of meters high; there are bacteria within us and within every living organism. Hyphae are found within the leaves and the fruits of the plants we eat, and up to ten different species of bacteria live in our navels, about twenty on our skin.

For the last 3.5 billion years, life has withdrawn most of the primitive atmospheric carbon dioxide.

Why?

One reason could be that as our planet ages, the amount of CO_2 degassing of its crust and mantle tends to diminish. In other words, the volcanic and other natural geological CO_2 springs that we analyzed in Chapter 8 are discharging today at a lower intensity than they were in the past. This could be related to the cooling of the Earth's mantle, a theory that is far from general consensus among earth science researchers.

A more realistic possibility is that the overall fall of the atmospheric CO_2 content is due to the combined effects of a lower geological degassing rate and a higher rate of carbon absorption by continental vegetation and cyanobacterial activity in the oceans.

In the last eight hundred thousand years, atmospheric CO_2 contents were on the verge of vegetation collapse, dangerously close to 180 ppm, but fortunately the geological degassing effect was still strong enough to reverse the cycle (see Table 5).

Very recently, during the Younger Dryas, the cause of a reversal back toward increasing levels of CO_2 in the atmosphere that stopped the progressive freezing was probably the result of human activity (Pausas & Keely, 2009): intentional fires related to proliferating hunting techniques or ecological changes resulting predatory activities that could have broken the balance between grass-feeding mammals, extending forests, or even wildfires unintentionally started by humans that hadn't yet mastered the consequences of their use of fire for cooking and wood hardening (Pyne, S.J., 2001).

From the roughly two quadrillion tons of CO_2 molecules that filled the primitive air, only less than two trillion are left.

Still, all life-forms depend on those two trillion.

But the life reaction is unidirectional; once started, it cannot stop. For eons, life has been removing carbon from the atmosphere, and it will proceed the same way until the amount of CO_2 in the future air will not be enough for plants to live.

Before the resulting doomsday of carbon dioxide starvation, the alchemy of evolution will provide new systems to improve CO_2 absorption even at meager concentrations. As it has done before with the creation of the C_4 plants, evolutionary mechanisms will provide new highly efficient plants capable of surviving even in the asphyxiating atmospheres of only 200 ppm of carbon dioxide.

But below that, below maybe 150–200 ppm, plants will first stop growing, then they will stop reproducing, and finally flowers will never blossom, and their seeds will never germinate.

Once the plants are dead, all the rest of us will follow, vanish, disappear.

We have a very short margin left; only 200 ppm (0.02 percent) separate our life-burgeoning planet from becoming an icy deserted landscape without biology.

ANNEX I: THE DECEPTIVE THEORY OF "OCEAN ACIDIFICATION"

Although papers, meetings and volumes are dedicated to "ocean acidification," with the exception of a few laboratory experiments (based on adding hydrochloric or similar acids to seawater in restricted environments), no one has ever demonstrated with real facts and figures that the oceans' pH have diminished in the last decades when compared to "preindustrial levels."

In our review of the recent scientific literature, hundreds to thousands of papers were found that have been published by the peer review boards of the most distinguished magazines, but yet they all ignore the most basic geological studies. Some of them imply rock units that were investigated by different teams of researchers in the most detailed and meticulous way. In brief, geological studies have demonstrated thousands of times that trillions of tons of coralline and other biogenic limestone were built in the past beneath oceans that were wrapped up by atmospheres containing anywhere from twice to a hundredfold more CO_2 than the present. And this happened for more than a billion years at all latitudes around the globe.

Let's have a quick look at some of the "jewels" recently published that reveal a total scientific ignorance of paleontology and geology:

A recent paper by Munday et al. (2012) tries to warn readers of the possibility that an elevated (400 ppm) CO_2 could have a "dramatic effect" on a wide range of behavioral and sensory responses among reef fish, with consequences for the timing of settlement, habitat selection, predator avoidance, and individual fitness.

Here is a quote from the abstract:

> Average sea-surface temperature and the amount of CO_2 dissolved in the ocean are rising as a result of increasing concentrations of atmospheric CO_2. Many coral reef fishes appear to be living close to their thermal optimum, and for some of them, even relatively moderate increases in temperature (2–4°C) lead to significant reductions in aerobic scope. Reduced aerobic capacity could affect population sustainability because less energy can be devoted to feeding and reproduction. Coral reef fishes seem to have limited capacity to acclimate to elevated temperature as adults, but recent research shows that developmental and transgenerational plasticity occur, which might enable some species to adjust to rising ocean temperatures. Predicted increases in **pCO_2, and associated ocean acidification, can also influence the aerobic scope of coral reef fishes**, although there is considerable interspecific variation, with some species exhibiting a decline and others an increase in aerobic scope at near-future CO_2 levels. As with thermal effects, there are transgenerational changes in response to elevated CO_2 that could mitigate impacts of high CO_2 on the growth and survival of reef fishes. An unexpected discovery is that **elevated CO_2 has a dramatic effect on a wide range of behaviors and sensory responses of reef fishes, with consequences for the timing of settlement, habitat selection, predator avoidance, and individual fitness. The underlying physiological mechanism appears to be the interference of acid-base regulatory processes with brain neurotransmitter function. Differences in the sensitivity of species and populations to global warming and rising CO_2 have been identified that will lead to changes in fish community structure**

as the oceans warm and becomes more acidic; however, the prospect for acclimation and adaptation of populations to these threats also needs to be considered. Ultimately, it will be the capacity for species to adjust to environmental change over coming decades that will determine the impact of climate change on marine ecosystems.

Here's another quote from an abstract from Pelejero et al. (2010):

The anthropogenic rise in atmospheric CO_2 is driving fundamental and **unprecedented** changes in the chemistry of the oceans. This has led to changes in the physiology of a wide variety of marine organisms and, consequently, the ecology of the ocean. This review explores recent advances in our understanding of ocean acidification with a particular emphasis on **past changes to ocean chemistry** and what they can tell us about present and future changes. We argue that ocean conditions are already **more ex-treme than those experienced by marine organisms and ecosystems for millions of years**, emphasizing the urgent need to adopt policies that drastically reduce CO_2 emissions.

Both Munday and Pelejero should borrow *Geology for Dummies* from the nearest library. If they did, they would learn how fish behaved (and survived) during five hundred million years under "elevated CO_2" (twenty times the current levels) conditions that, indeed, were that "extreme" during millions of years.

Let's now have a look at Guinotte and Fabry (2008) abstract:

Ocean acidification is rapidly changing the carbonate system of the world oceans. Past mass extinction events have been linked to ocean acidification, and the current rate of change in seawater chemistry is unprecedent.

The only problem here is that:

- Ocean acidification is unproved
- No past mass extinction events have been linked to ocean acidification
- No current rate of change in sea water chemistry has been proved

One has to wonder how shell-building marine creatures and these other fish survived for more than five hundred million years in those acidic oceans. How did calcium carbonate stromatolites develop in shallow seas under 1 percent (10,000 ppm) CO_2 atmosphere?

Caldeira and Wickett's (2003) paper is repeatedly used as an argument to justify "ocean acidification." Quoting from its abstract:

> *The coming centuries may see more ocean acidification than the past **300 million years**. Most carbon dioxide released into the atmosphere as a result of the burning of fossil fuels will eventually be absorbed by the ocean, with potentially adverse consequences for marine biota. Here we quantify the changes in ocean pH that may result from this continued release of CO2 and compare these with pH changes estimated from geological and historical records.*

The most incredible argument comes in the last paragraph of their abstract:

> *We find that oceanic absorption of CO2 from fossil fuels may result in larger pH changes over the next several centuries than any inferred from the **geological record of the past 300 million years**, with the possible exception of those resulting from rare, extreme events such as bolide impacts or catastrophic methane hydrate degassing.*

How can both authors ignore that three hundred million years ago, the atmospheric CO_2 content was 2,000 ppm, or five times the current levels?

A paper by Hoegh-Guldberg et al. (2007) is also often referred on the subject of ocean acidification. But this is another case of "**expect-ed** conditions" for the immediate future and is solely based on wishful thinking with no **experimental data** or historical records to prove the "expected acidification."

Quoting their abstract:

> Atmospheric carbon dioxide concentration **is expected** to exceed 500 parts per million and global temperatures to rise by at least 2°C by 2050 to 2100, values that significantly exceed those of at least the past 420,000 years during which most extant marine organisms evolved. Under conditions expected in the 21st century, global warming and **ocean acidi-fication will compromise carbonate accretion, with corals becoming increasingly rare on reef systems. The result will be less diverse reef communities and carbonate reef structures that fail to be maintained.** Climate change also exacerbates local stresses from declining water quality and overexploitation of key species, driving reefs increasingly toward the tipping point for functional collapse. This review presents future scenarios for coral reefs that predict increasingly serious consequences for reef-associated fisheries, tourism, coastal protection, and people. As the International Year of the Reef 2008 begins, scaled-up management intervention and decisive action on global emissions are required if the loss of coral-dominated ecosystems is to be avoided.

Same comments as above.

J. E. N. Veron published a weird paper in 2008 in which he defines five extinction events affecting coral reefs and claims that two of those (the almost universal extinctions of the Permian/Triassic and Cretaceous/Tertiary) were the result of ocean acidification in association with high levels of CO_2 in the atmosphere. Following these assumptions, he concludes that a sixth mass extinction of corals is about to occur as a result of the current levels of atmospheric CO_2. But there is no scientific proof that any of the extinctions were due to ocean acidification. This "acidification theory of extinction" cannot explain why the dinosaurs, which neither bathed nor surfed near the "acidic" beaches at the end of the Cretaceous, became extinct at the same time as scalded ammonites.

Based on this type of nonexperimental data, which is sustained by guesses or "projected changes," and which also assumes that deviations in pH effects are a result of the "postindustrial" increase of atmospheric CO_2, the Royal Society (2005) published an update entitled *"Ocean Acidification Due to Increasing Carbon Dioxide. Policy Document 12/05,"* which was written in coordination with several fellow scientists from assorted science areas. This document is also based on an overview of "potential consequences" without the support of any data or measurement showing that there is an oceanic acidification process in course.

Surprisingly, it is worth underlining that, contrary to all arguments as exemplified above, some papers describe experimental results indicating that in some cases **seawater acidification increases calcification**.

In a 2008 paper, Iglesias-Rodriguez describes the experiments performed in the case of coccolithophore organisms (accounting for about a third of the total marine calcium carbonate production), which show that calcification and photosynthesis both *increased by up to 40 percent* under elevated CO_2, while it remained unchanged for other species.

Pandolfi (2011) at least considers that all variables must be taken into account and thoroughly studied and tested before making adventurous claims into future disastrous outcomes.

THE VARIABILITY OF OCEAN pH

The fact is that the surface waters of the oceans show a broad variation in pH, depending on seasons, proximity to land masses, and the effect of upwelling currents. Although the average pH value is 8.1, fluctuations between 7.9 and 8.5 have been measured in different instances.

As was mentioned before, most of the proponents of ocean acidification theories do not take the biological factor into account in their calculations. Everything is based on future projected amounts of CO_2 in the atmosphere and its corresponding CO_2 increase when dissolved in ocean waters. Life is always taken as a neutral and never as an influential term in their equations.

But indeed there are hundreds of papers describing biomineralization of calcium or magnesium carbonate tests, shells, exoskeletons, bacterial mats, and straight precipitation built by water creatures under extreme environments, whether in acidic, anoxic, high-temperature, or high-pressure.

Deep hydrothermal vents are a classic dramatic example not only of life growing under "inferno" conditions but also the microorganisms' ability to construct limestone (calcium and magnesium carbonates) out of either dissolved CO_2 in the seawater or by transformation of methane and sulfates in the case of submarine cold seeps. The deep, anoxic waters of the Black Sea are prolific in these kinds of methane cold seeps and the precipitation of authigenic carbonates, in many cases materializing as limestone columns of several feet height.

Ehrlich and Newman's book, *Geomicrobiology* (2008), is filled with numerous examples of bacterial precipitation of calcium and magnesium carbonate under the most extremely varied chemical conditions.

On the other side, if one takes into account the fact that Earth's rivers and lakes, all with normal pH levels of 7 or lower (slightly acidic), are populated with a rich fauna of nearly a thousand different species of mollusks and other carbonated tests organisms, one cannot find a compelling reason for marine invertebrates to withstand a lowered pH in oceanic waters. Actually, the zebra mussel (*Dreissena polymorpha*), a freshwater mollusk native to the Caspian seawaters, is famous today for its widespread invasion of European rivers, channels, reservoirs, harbors, and even water pipes and the cooling towers of power generator stations, regardless of water pH.

It is also a well-established fact that the lowest-pH oceanic waters are found in the upheaval areas, where the highest organic productivity is located. Would that mean that, in fact, as was found by

Iglesias-Rodriguez (2008), the CO_2-enriched seawaters *increase* marine calcium carbonate fixation, promoting a swarm of microplankton?

Moreover, exceptional scientific studies like the one published by Evans et al. in *Molecular Ecology* (2013) describe the capacity of purple sea urchins (*Strongylocentrotus purpuratus*) to withstand seawaters within a pH range between 8.1 and 7.6. This last relatively "acidic" pH is related to upwelling in coastal Oregon (as the reader should probably know, urchins have big, thick endoskeletons made of calcium carbonate). More studies relating the resilience of marine organisms to changes in seawater acidity will probably appease the current hysteria surrounding oceanic acidification.

The ultimate argument against the ocean acidification deception was presented by Liu (2011) using the Boron-11 isotope in fossil corals to reconstruct the pH variations for the South China Sea in the last seven thousand years and showing that, during that time, the pH of the seawaters oscillated between 7.9 and 8.3, with the lowest pH estimate of 7.9 at about 6,000 YBP.

As was shown by 3.5 billion years of geological history, water acidity or alkalinity is an irrelevant albeit functional factor for the development of calcareous tests and related limestone deposits.

ANNEX II: THE THREAT OF A NEW ICE AGE

After the Second World War, scientists noticed a cooling trend in average world temperatures, an event that was credited to the increase of human air pollution and the resulting opacity of the atmosphere, which may have been reducing the incoming sunlight.

Rassol and Schneider presented a paper in *Science* magazine in 1971 speculating that, in spite of the atmospheric CO_2 increase, the increase of aerosol density was strong enough to dim the solar radiation, and as a consequence, a new Little Ice Age (1560–1715) could be triggered as a result of human industrial pollution.

Later, in 1976, the columnist Lowell Ponte presented a book called *The Cooling* that for a few months was at the top of the best seller's lists. This three-hundred-page book is a journalistic analysis devoid of any sort of scientific references; but in a way, it reflects the prevailing academic tendency in the late sixties and early seventies when most of weather scientists believed in a future cooling of the planet rather than the later shift toward warming and CO_2 anthropogenic climate change.

Before that, in November 1969, the prestigious meteorologist Dr. J. Murray Mitchell Jr. warned about global cooling worries in an article published in *Science News* magazine:

"How long the current cooling trend continues is one of the most important problems of our civilization."

"The threat of a new ice age must now stand alongside nuclear war as a likely source of wholesale death and misery for mankind," said

Nigel Calder in a 1970 interview that was followed by a 1974 article in *Nature*. This former editor of the *New Scientist* magazine strongly argues for a coming global cooling, a belief that he still maintains at his eighty-three years of age.

In a report presented to the National Academy of Sciences in January 1975, C. C. Wallen, then Chief of the Special Environmental Applications Division and representing the United States for the World Meteorological Organization, declared that, *"The cooling since 1940 has been large enough and consistent enough that it will not be reversed...we may be approaching the end of a major interglacial cycle with the approach of a full-blown, ten thousand–year ice age, a real possibility."*

Professor Hubert Horace Lamb (1913–1997), the founder of the Climate Research Unit at the University of East Anglia in 1972 and author of myriad scientific papers and two famous books on climate history (*Climate: Present, Past, and Future [1972]* and *Climate, History, and the Modern World [1995]*), stated:

"The last twenty years of this century (1980 to 2000) will be progressively colder."

According to the CIA in a 1974 study entitled *Study of Climatological Research as it Pertains to Intelligence Problems*, reads: *"The new climatic era (cooling) brings a promise of famine and starvation to many areas of the world."*

George Kukla (1930-2014) was a Czech geologist that chose to live in the United States in the early seventies. He and Robert Matthews of Brown University both became outstanding supporters of the global cooling hypothesis. Kukla published an impressive amount of papers in well-known peer-reviewed magazines such as *Science*, the *Geological Society of America Bulletin*, and *Quaternary Research*, where he makes the point on geological evidence showing the high frequency of glacial intervals during the last million years of Earth's history, as well as the influence of temperature measurement bias as a result of urbanization around measuring stations (Karl, Kukla et al. 1991).

Walter O. R. Roberts (1915–1990) was a Harvard astronomer working for the NOAA at Boulder, Colorado, as well as the founder of the National Center for Atmospheric Research. He maintained in several of his papers dealing with solar corpuscular emissions that the sun's activity is paramount in controlling the terrestrial cloud cover. In a 1973 paper, he stated that due to the effects of the sun's activity on the troposphere that results from aurora-induced cirrus clouds over the relatively warm Gulf of Alaska, the Earth "may have entered a new *Little Ice Age*."

Don J. Easterbrook, an emeritus professor at Western Washington University, is a strong supporter of a coming intense global cooling that will affect growing and harvest seasons, causing a dramatic fall in food production. In his book, *Evidence-Based Climate Science* (Elsevier 2011), he relates the future freezing to a coming solar cycle of significantly reduced sunspots. Easterbrook is an expert in recent glaciology and has published an impressive amount of scientific papers, mainly in the *Bulletin of the Geological Society of America.*

H. Abdussamatov puts the start of the next freezing wave in the present, 2014, with temperatures dropping several degrees to reach their lowest point by 2055. This Russian scientist—a member of the Russian Academy of Sciences and the head of the Pulkovo Space Research Laboratory in St. Petersburg—believes that the sharp drop in temperature will start in 2014, and as are many others scientists, he is a devout believer in climate oscillations triggered by the variation in sunspot activity. In his 2013 paper: *Grand Minimum of the Total Solar Irradiance leds to the Little Ice Age* he states that in a few years we will watch the same scenarios that were already seen before, like the last four-day freezing of the Thames in London in 1814 (which was nothing compared to the Great Frost of 1683–84, when the ice lasted for almost two months), or the freezing of the Hudson River in New York in January 1821.

But Abdussamatov is not alone. According to Professor M. Lockwood of Reading University, the *Little Ice Age*, which extended approximately between 1560 and 1715, was caused by the Maunder Minimum that occurred between 1645 and 1715 when the sun was showing only fifty spots on its surface, compared to the normal rate of near fifty thousand spots per year (Jones, Lockwood & Stott, 2012).

Another one is Richard A. Muller, an old skeptic on global warming and the current director of the Berkeley Earth Project. In 1995, together with G. J. MacDonald, Muller proposed that glaciations are triggered by slight periodical oscillations of the Earth's orbit that penetrate into an area of dense cosmic dust that intercepts the Earth's atmosphere, resulting in an enhancement of cloud formation and increase of the planet's albedo.

Timothy Patterson is also convinced that a new ice age is approaching. Tim is a Canadian professor of Geology at Carleton University that has authored several papers showing the present close relation between solar cycles and Holocene sea bottom cores from deep West Canadian fjords. He expects that an extreme cooling season will start around 2018, seriously affecting Canadian agriculture (Patterson, T., 2005).

Based on a similar hypothesis, Shaviv and Veizer (2003) sustain that Earth's climate is controlled by both the effects of the increasing CO_2 concentration in the atmosphere and the galactic cosmic ray flux (CRF) variability, which is itself linked to the solar system's passage through the spiral arms of the galaxy, increasing cloud formation and albedo.

A similar theory was offered by Paul LaViolette from the University of Arizona in 2011, which shows evidences for a solar flare as the triggering cause for the Pleistocene mass extinction.

ANNEX III: ICE AGE

Mammuthus trogontherii appeared in Europe and Asia 750,000 YBP (more or less in coincidence with the start of the Quaternary Glacial periods) as a kind of woolly elephant well adapted to cold. Although quite impressive for its long and arched tusks, the main difference between this animal and the rest of the elephant family is in its teeth. The mammoth's teeth were perfectly adapted to the rather tough grasses and shrubs that grew in the cold steppes of the northern hemisphere. But in fact this species was an intermediate stage to the more cold-adapted *Mammuthus primigenius* that started to roam a larger area, extending from the present Alaska and Canada to most of Europe (down to Madrid, Spain), Russia, and Siberia much later, around 250,000 YBP. Their number must have been enormous, as can be deduced by its impact caused on Neanderthal and Cro-Magnon people who repeatedly painted the animals' silhouettes in caves. Frozen remains of mammoths in the permafrost soils of Siberia and Alaska are also numerous, especially if we take into account the fact that thousands of tusks were ripped from the ice during centuries of ivory trade, which was probably even more extensive before the trade began to be documented in the seventeenth century.

Mammoth remains are key to understanding the big glaciations, their extent, their duration, and very specifically the speed of the temperature drop. Normally, the soft tissues of mammals start to decay a few hours after death, with both the cellular enzymes and bacteria starting to break proteins down into simpler molecules. Liquid water is essential in the process, so that preservation can be generated by complete desiccation (like in the case of the Andean mummies), or by freezing. The quicker the freezing process takes place, the better the preserved outcome, but also the temperature drop must be as rapid as possible to avoid the formation of ice needles that could destroy the cellular membranes. This, of course, is volume-related, so that while a sudden drop to minus thirty degrees centigrade is necessary for a cattle-size carcass, a drop of at least thirty-five degrees in a matter of a few minutes would be necessary to preserve a whole mammoth body, including its digestive system.

The Beresovka mammoth was the first relatively intact animal recovered by an Austrian science expedition led by O. Herz and E. Pfizenmeyer in 1901. After four months of travelling, they reached the remains of the carcass in the banks of the Beresovka River, near the Arctic Sea coast. Most of its head and upper trunk had been eaten by wolves, but the rest was well preserved, including some of the grass still imprisoned in its grinding teeth. Unfortunately, they had to defrost the body to prepare its transportation before freezing it again, a practice that could have spoiled most of the mammoth's delicate organs. The present freezing wasn't very complicated. In those last days before their departure, the local temperature was hovering around negative forty-five degrees centigrade. Today, the Beresovka mammoth is conserved unspoiled and frozen at the St. Petersburg Academy of Sciences. The animal was found on its haunches, an indication that he was mired in mud at the moment of his death. Its stomach was full of grass, signifying that it wasn't a case of starvation.

The Shandrin mammoth was found in 1972, with its stomach almost totally filled with mainly grasses and sedges, the rest a mass of twigs, tips, leaves, and willow, larch, and birch bark. Similar diets were confirmed from the stomach contents of frozen woolly rhinoceroses and horses. Today, those grass-covered steppes don't exist in the same area, being replaced by grassless tundra (where only mosses and lichens grow) or the pine tree forests that carpet the taiga farther south.

Bernard Buigues is a French explorer and entrepreneur that lives in Khatanga (Russia), five hundred miles north of the Arctic Circle. Together with other scientists like Yves Copens, Alexei Tikhonov, and Dan Fisher, he created a foundation several years ago named

Mammuthus, whose mission is to search, conserve, and study Siberian mammoth remains (visit www.mammuthus.org to learn more). As a result, they have already found seven frozen carcasses.

Markel, discovered in 1996, as well as Jarkov in 1999, was a forty-six-year-old mammoth that died twenty thousand years ago. The incomplete remains of another mammoth, Fish Hook, were located in 2001. Yukagir, a forty-eight-year-old animal that died 18,500 years ago, was found in 2003. Lyuba, a female calf only thirty-one days old that still had breast milk in its stomach, was found in 2007. Khroma, another baby mammoth that died 45,000 YBP, was encountered in 2009. Together with those mammoths, a number of frozen remains of horses, elk, musk, oxen, and wolves were also located during the exploration campaigns. Cherskyi is the name of the most complete carcass of a woolly rhinoceros ever found.

ANNEX IV: CO$_2$ EMISSIONS FROM UNCONTROLLED CARBON FIRES

The United States has nearly a hundred naturally occurring underground fires extending from Alaska to Alabama, with Pennsylvania being the most notable location, where the Centralia mine fire has been burning since 1962. Although all sorts of methods were tried to extinguish it, nothing has proven effective, and after a few days of dropping smoke and heat, the fires would restart with renewed ferocity (Krajick 2005).

The Federal Office of Surface Mining keeps a database with all the recorded coal fires in the United States, which fortunately dropped from 150 locations in 1999 to only one hundred by the end of 2010, although some geologists sustain that many more fires remain unrecorded. In Pennsylvania alone, some forty-five fires have been documented, while in some areas of Colorado, the coal fires ignite whenever the groundwater table subsides during drought periods and later is naturally quenched by heavy rain spells.

The old New Castle coal mine in Garfield County, Colorado, was fully active in 1896 when an explosion due to methane gas killed forty-nine miners. Since then, the coal seams have burned, sometimes with unusual ferocity, destroying buildings and forcing the evacuation of certain suburbs. In New Straitsville, an abandoned coal mine has been burning since 1884, when a riot started during a miner strike, triggering an underground fire that still melts the winter snow on the surface.

Underground coal, lignite, and peat fires can start spontaneously over outcropped or exposed beds rich in carbon contents, simply as a result of sulfur oxidation under a dry spell, as periodically happens in Mali at the peat deposits of the abandoned Niger meanders near Timbuktu or the recent fires in Yemen. Coalfaces or galleries resulting from abandoned mines and exposed to weathering and oxidation can also start fires with flame fronts that move along the coal bed underneath. Of course, fires can be also started by a surface forest or brush fire, or even by lighting. Once the fire extends downward, it is almost impossible to control without drowning the old galleries with water, which could cause serious damage to inhabited areas.

Stracher (2007) observes that China and India are the champions of underground fires as a result of unregulated mining practices such as superficial, hand-dug holes that are abandoned when the cavities go too deep. These holes can be numbered by the thousands in a relatively small area and produce intensive air passages that contribute to spontaneous oxidation. In 2010, an estimated sixty-eight fires were burning in the Jharia coalfield in India, where the first fire started in 1916 and which has become a sixty-square-mile wasteland today.

But nothing compares to the current situation in Indonesia (Stracher 2011), where extensive areas that used to be covered by rain forests were first logged and then cleared for agriculture by slash-and-burn methods that easily produced the kindling for an outcropping coal beds and old peat deposits. This practice has triggered thousands of coal fires, destroying entire villages and producing heavy smoke carpets that extended over much of Southeast Asia, blocking out sunlight, causing crop failures, reducing visibility, and producing serious health consequences. Recent satellite surveys estimate that more than 250,000 coal seam and peat fires have been burning in Indonesia since 1998.

It is estimated that Australia's Burning Mountain is the oldest known active coal fire, which has been smoking for six thousand years, while a coal seam located near the city of Zwickau in Germany burned for nearly four centuries between 1476 and 1860. On the contrary, the Dudweiler coal seam in the Saar region is still burning today after it ignited in 1668. Old lignite opencast mines in Germany have been burning for centuries and are considered more tourist attractions than calamities. The scientific team of the Lewis and Clark Expedition was the first to record and describe the lignite fires in the Powder River Basin in Wyoming and Montana in 1804. Later geological studies found evidence that some of the coal fires there started three million years ago.

Of course, Great Britain, with its long history of more than three centuries of coal mining, has witnessed a large number of underground coal fires, some of them with tragic results. The more recent one happened in the Daw Mill colliery (about ten miles east of Birmingham). This coal mine was scheduled to cease production by the end of 2013, the last coal mine to produce in Warwickshire and one of the very few remaining active mines in the UK. But about a year before the closure, in February 2013, a ferocious underground fire suddenly started on an old coalface 1,770 feet below the surface, burning to an extent unseen in the last fifty years. The fire demanded the immediate evacuation of roughly a hundred miners, who were unaffected by the accident, which prompted the early closure of the pit.

Coal seams, lignites, or peat fires, whether active or relic, are verified in many places around the world, such as in the Strongman Mine on the west coast of New Zealand or the Witbank collieries in the Transvaal region of South Africa. Coal and lignite fires have also been reported in Colombia, Brazil, Egypt, Turkey, Thailand, Poland, France, and Portugal.

Several examples of coal fires that burned in the geological past can be seen in the Cerrejon Coal Mine in Colombia, one of the largest open-pit coal mines in the world. The heat produced by the combustion transformed the clay content of the coal beds into a red clinker mass up to 330 feet thick. These clinker masses are mostly related to old faulted areas that hindered the water and oxygen penetration into the coal seam and thus triggered the spontaneous oxidation-combustion. Although the current coal mined at Cerrejon is of low sulfur and ash content, the layers that burned in the past were richer in both clay and pyrite contents.

A famous fire registered in the summer of 2010 during a forty-degree centigrade heat wave in Central Russia ignited thick peat deposits, burning thousands of houses and blanketing the area with a dense toxic smoke. At the end of August, the toxic fumes reached Moscow, putting the city on the verge of a possible mass evacuation.

In North America, peat fires can occur during severe droughts, from boreal forests in Canada to swamps in the subtropical southern Florida wetlands, like the famous everglade bayous. Once a fire has burned through the area, hollows in the peat are burnt out, though desiccated hummocks can contribute to peat-building vegetation recolonization.

Research results from the International Institute for Geo-Information Science and Earth Observation in the Netherlands suggest that nearly two hundred million tons of coal are consumed in the world every year as a result of spontaneous combustion, an equivalent to the amount of coal imported by Japan in the recent years.

Based on data released by the Chinese Central Mining Institute, which reanalyzed information gathered by remote sensing satellite computations, Van Dijk (2011) estimates that in situ coal combustion in China represents about 0.2 percent of the global fossil fuel–related CO_2 emissions. But taking into account the importance of coal fires in Indonesia and India, the global figure for CO_2 emissions resulting from uncontrolled coal seams, lignite, and peat could easily represent somewhere between 2 and 3 percent of human-related CO_2 emissions, especially when considering that most smoldering peat fires can burn undetected for many decades.

Some scientists believe that anywhere from twenty to two hundred million tons of fossil fuels such as coal seams, lignite deposits, and peatlands burn each year—depending on dry spells and other weather-related variables. On the average, this produces the above indicated percentages of the total carbon dioxide from fossil fuels burned on earth.

Even so and according to figures published by the United Nations Environmental Program in 1999 (Levine), peat and forest fires in Indonesia released between 0.8 and 2.6×10^9 tons of carbon, which is equivalent to somewhere between 13 and 40 percent of the total carbon released by fossil fuel burning.

REFERENCES

Abdussamatov, Habibullo I. 2013. *Grand Minimum of the Total Solar Irradiance Leads to the Little Ice Age.* Journal of Geology and Geosciences, 2(113)

Adams, J. M., and H. Faure. 1998. *The Global Atlas of Paleovegetation Since the Last Glacial Maximum.* Environmental Science Division, Oak Ridge National Laboratory. Retrieved from www.esd.ornl.gov/project/adams.

Ainsworth, Elizabeth A., and Stephen P. Long. 2005. *What Have we Learned from 15 years of Free-Air CO_2 Enrichment (FACE)? A Meta-Analytic Review of the Responses of Photosynthesis, Canopy Properties, and Plant Production to Rising CO_2.* The New Phytologist, 165(2): 351–71. doi: 10.1111/j.1469-8137.

Allard, Patrick, M. Burton, N. Oskarsson, A. Michel, and M. Polacci. 2011. *Magmatic gas composition and fluxes during the 2010 Eyjafjallajökull explosive eruption: implications for degassing magma volumes and volatile sources.* Geophysical Research Abstract, 13. 2010AGUFM. V53F.07A

Allen, Hartwel L., E. C. Bisbal, K. J. Boote and P. H. Jones et al. 1991. *Soybean Dry Matter Allocation Under Subambient and Superambient Levels of Carbon Dioxide.* Agronomy Journal, 83: 875–83. doi: 10.2134agronj/00021962008300050020x

Allwood, Abigail C., M.R. Walter, I.W. Burch and B.S. Kamber. 2007. *The 3.43 Billion-Year-Old Strelley Pool Chert, Pilbara Craton, Western Australia: Ecosystem-Scale Insights to Early Life on Earth*. Precambrian Research 158(3): 198–227.

Balée, W.L., and C.L. Erickson. 2006. *Time and Complexity in Historical Ecology—Studies in the Neotropical Lowlands*. New York: Columbia University Press, Barichivich, Jonathan, K.R. Briffa, R.B. Myneni, T.J. Osborn, T.M. Melvin, P. Ciais, S. Piao and C. Tucker 2013. *"Large Scale Variations in the Vegetation Growing Season and Annual Cycle of Atmospheric CO_2 of High Northern Latitudes from 1950 to 2011."* Global Change Biology, 19(10): 3167–83. doi: 10.1111/gcb.12283

Bates, Nicholas R., S.B. Moran, D.A. Hansell, and J.T. Mathis 2006. *"An Increasing CO_2 Sink in the Arctic Ocean Due to Sea-Ice Loss."* Geophysical Research Letters 33(23):609. doi:10.1029/2006gl027028

Beerling, David J., L.L. Taylor, C.D.C. Bradshaw, D.J. Lunt, P.J. Valdes, S.A. Banwart, M. Pagani and J.R. Leake. 2012. *"Ecosystem CO_2 Starvation and Terrestrial Silicate Weathering: Mechanisms and Global-Scale Quantification during the Late Miocene*. Journal of Ecology, 100: 31–41. doi: 10.1111/j.1365-2745.2011.01905.x

Berner, R. A., and Z. Kothavala. 2001. *"Geocarb III: A Revised Model of Atmospheric CO_2 Over Phanerozoic Time."* American Journal of Science, 301: 182–204.

Bloom, Arnold J., M. Burger, B.A. Kimball & P.J. Pinter, Jr. 2014. *"Nitrate Assimilation is Inhibited by Elevated CO_2 in Field-Grown Wheat."* Nature Climate Change 4: 477–480. doi:10.1038/nclimate2183

Brodo, I. M., S. D. Sharnoff & S. Sharnoff. 2001. *Lichens of North America*. Yale University Press, New Haven and London. 795 pp.

Buick, R., Rasmussen, B., Krapez, B., 1998. *Archean oil: evidence for extensive hydrocarbon generation and migration 2.5-3.5 Ga.* American Association of Petroleum Geologists Bulletin 82, 50-69

Caldeira, K. and M. E. Wickett. 2003. *Oceanography: Anthropogenic Carbon and Ocean pH.* Nature, 425 (365).

Calder, Nigel. 1974. *"The Arithmetic of Ice Ages."* Nature, 252: 216–218. doi:10.1038/252216a0

Carbon Dioxide Information Analysis Center (CDIAC). 2012. *800,000 Year Ice Core Records of Atmospheric Carbon Dioxide.* US Department of Energy. Office of Science. Oak Ridge National Laboratory

Cerling, T. E., J. R Ehleringer, and J. M. Harris. 1998. *Carbon Dioxide Starvation, the Development of C4 Ecosystems and Mammalian Evolution.* Philosophical Transactions of the Royal Society B, Biological Sciences, 353 (1365): 159–70. doi: 10.1098/rstb.1998.0198

Challinor A, J., J. Watson, D.B. Lobell, S.M. Howden, D.R. Smith and N. Chhetri. 2014. *A meta-analysis of crop yield under climate change and adaptation*, Nature Climate Change, 4:287-291. doi: 10.1038/nclimate2153

Chiodini, G., F. Frondini, C. Cardellini, F. Parello and L. Peruzzi. 2000. *Rate of Diffuse Carbon Dioxide Earth Degassing Estimated from Carbon Balance of Regional Aquifers: The Case of Central Apennine, Italy.* Journal of Geophysical Research, 105 (B4): 8423–8434. DOI: 10.1029/1999JB900355

Christner, B. C., C. E. Morris, C. M. Foreman, R. Cai, and D. C. Sands. 2008. *Ubiquity of Biological Ice Nucleators in Snowfall.* Science, 319: 1214.

Cripps, I., P. Munday, and M. I. McCormick. 2011. *Ocean Acidification Affects Prey Detection by a Predatory Reef Fish.* PLoS One, 6 (7): 1–7.

Dadachova, E., and A. Casadevall. 2008. *Ionizing Radiation: How Fungi Cope, Adapt, and Exploit with the Help of Melanin.* Current Opinion In Microbiology, 1(6): 525–531.

DeLeon-Rodriguez, Natasha et al. 2013. *Microbiome of the Upper Troposphere: Species Composition and Prevalence, Effects of Tropical Storms, and Atmospheric Implications.* Proceedings of the National Academy of Sciences,110(7):2575–80.doi: 10.1073/pnas.1212089110

De'ath, G., J. M. Lough, and K. E. Fabricius. 2009. *Declining Coral Calcification on the Great Barrier Reef.* Science, 323: 116–19.

Dippery, J. K., D.T. Tissue, R.B. Thomas and B.R. Strain. 1995. *Effects of low and elevated CO_2 on C_3 and C_4 annuals. I: Growth and Biomass Allocation."* Oecologia, 101: 13–20.

Donovan, L. A., and J. R. Ehleringer. 1991. *Ecophysiological Differences Among Juvenile and Reproductive Plants of Several Woody Species.* Oecologia, 86: 594–97.

Drake, B. G., and P. W. Leadley. 1991. *Canopy Photosynthesis of Crops and Native Plant Communities Exposed to Long-Term Elevated CO_2.* Plant, Cell & Environment, 14 (8): 853–60.

Easterbrook, D. J. 2011. *Evidence-Based Climate Science.* Elsevier Publishers, Amsterdam, Netherlands.

Ehleringer, J. R., T. E. Cerling, and D. M. Dearing (eds.). 2005. *A History of Atmospheric CO_2 and Its Effects on Plants, Animals, and Ecosystems.* Springer Verlag, New York.

Ehleringer, J. R., T. E. Cerling, and B. E. Helliker. 1997. *C_4 Photosynthesis, Atmospheric CO_2, and Climate.* Oecologia, 112: 285–89.

Ehrlich, H. L. and D. K. Newman. 2008. *Geomicrobiology.* Boca Raton, CRC Press.

Eklundh, L., and L. Olssson. 2003. *Vegetation Index Trends for the African Sahel 1982–1999.* Geophysical Research Letters, 30 (8).

Evans, T. G., F. Chan, B. A. Menge, and G. E. Hofmann. 2013. *Transcriptomic Responses to Ocean Acidification in Larval Sea Urchins from a Naturally Variable pH Environment.* Molecular Ecology, 22 (6): 1609–1625. doi: 10.1111/mec.12188

Filippov, M.M.. 2002. *Shungite rocks of the Onega structure.* Karelian Research Center, Report N°280 (in Russian)

Finsinger, W., and F. Wagner. 2009. *Stomatal-Based Inference Models for Reconstruction of Atmospheric CO_2 Concentration: A Method Assessment Using a Calibration and Validation Approach.* Holocene, 19 (5): 757–764.

Firestone, R. B. et al. 2007. *Evidence for an Extraterrestrial Impact 12,900 Years Ago, That Contributed to the Megafaunal Extinction and Younger Dryas Cooling.* Proceedings of the National Academy of Sciences, 104: 16016–21.

Fröhlich-Nowoisky, Janine, D.A. Pickersgill, A. Deprés, R. Viviane and U. Pösch. 2009. *High Diversity of Fungi in Air Particulate Matter.* Proceedings of the National Academy of Sciences, 106(31): 12814–19.

Gauthier-Lafaye, F. 2006. *Time Constraint for the Occurrence of Uranium Deposits and Natural Nuclear Fission Reactors in the Paleoproterozoic Franceville Basin (Gabon). IN Evolution of the Earth's Early Atmosphere, Hydrosphere, and Biosphere: Constraints from Ore Deposits.* Edited by H. Ohmoto and S. E. Kesler, 157–67. Boulder: Geological Society of America Special Volume, 198.

Gerhart, Laci M., and J. K. Ward. 2010. *Plant Responses to Low CO_2 of the Past.* The New Phytologist, 188(3): 674–695. doi: 10.1111/ j. 1469-8137.2010.03441.x

Ghori, K.A.R., J. Craig, B. Thusu, S. Lüning and M. Geiger. 2009. *Global Infracambrian Petroleum Systems: A Review*. Special Publications, 326: 109–36. London: Geological Society.

Guinotte, J. M. and V. J. Fabry. 2008. *Ocean Acidification and its Potential Effects on Marine Ecosystems*. Annals of the New York Academy of Sciences, 1134: 320–342. doi: 10.1196/annals.1439.013.

Gifford, R. M. 1992. *Interaction of Carbon Dioxide with Growth-Limiting Environmental Factors in Vegetation Productivity: Implications for the Global Carbon Cycle*. Advances in Bioclimatology, 1: 24–58.

Gradstein, Felix M. et al. 2012. *The Geologic Time Scale 2012*. Edited by Felix M. Gradstein, James G. Ogg, Mark D. Schmitz and Gabi M. Ogg. Published by Elsevier B.V. DOI: 10.1016/B978-0-444-59425-9.01001-5

Guthrie, D. R. 1990. *Frozen Fauna of the Mammoth Steppe. The Story of Blue Babe*. The University of Chicago Press.

Hards, V.L.. 2005. *Volcanic contributions to the global carbon cycle*. Nottingham, UK, British Geological Survey, 20pp. (British Geological Survey Occasional Publication, 10).

Hicks, M. and S. M. Rowland. 2004. *The Early Cambrian Experiment in Reef-Building by Metazoans: A Cambrian Biological Revolution*. Short Course in Paleontology, Denver, Colorado.

Hicks, M. and S. M. Rowland. 2009. *Early Cambrian Microbial Reefs, Archaeocyathan Inter-Reef Communities, and Associated facies of the Yangtze Platform*. Palaeogeography, Palaeoclimatology, Palaeoecology, 281 (1–2): 137–53.

Hillier, J. K. and A. B. Watts. 2007. *Global Distribution of Seamounts from Ship-Track Bathymetry Data*. Geophysical Research Letters, 34(13), 5pp.

Hoegh-Guldberg, Ove et al. 2007. *Coral Reefs Under Rapid Climate Change and Ocean Acidification.* Science, 318: 1737–42. doi:10.1126/science.1152509

Idso, C. D., and K. E. Idso. 2000. *Forecasting World Food Supplies: The Impact of the Rising Atmospheric CO_2 Concentration.* Technology, 7S: 33–55.

Idso, S. B., C. D. Idso., and K. E. Idso. 2003. *Enhanced or Impaired? Human Health in a CO_2-Enriched Warmer World.* Center for the Study of Carbon Dioxide and Global Change.

Iglesias-Rodriguez, M. Débora et al. 2008. *Phytoplankton Calcification in a High-CO_2 World.* Science, 18 (320): 336–40. doi:10.1126/science.1154122

IPPC, 4th *Assessment Report. 2007. Intergovernamental Panel on Climate Change. IPPC,* Geneva, Switzerland

Jones, Gareth S., M. Lockwood and P.A. Stott. 2012. *What influence will future solar activity changes over the 21st century have on projected global near-surface temperature changes?* Journal of Geophysical Research: Atmospheres, 117 (D5) doi: 10.1029/2011JD017013

Karl, Thomas. R., G. Kukla, V. Razuvayev, M.J. Changery, R.G. Quayle, R. Heim Jr., D. R. Easterling and C.B. Fu. 1991. *Global warming: evidence for asymmetric diurnal temperature change.* Geophysical Research Letters, 18 (12): 2253–2256. doi: 10.1029/91gl02900

Kaplan Michael R., J.M. Schaefer, G.H. Denton, D.J.A. Barrell, T.J.H. Chinn, A.E. Putnam, B.G. Andersen, R.C. Finkel, R. Schwartz & A.M. Doughty. 2010. *Glacier Retreat in New Zealand During the Younger Dryas Stadial.* Nature, 467 (7312): 194–195. doi:10.1038/nature09313

Kaufman Alan J. and Xiao Shuhai. 2003. *High CO_2 Levels in the Proterozoic Atmosphere Estimated from Analyses of Individual Microfossils.* Nature,425:279–82. doi:10.1038/nature01902

Keeling, Charles D., J.F.S. Chin & T.P. Whorf. 1996. *Increased Activity of Northern Vegetation Inferred from Atmospheric CO₂ Measurements.* Nature, 382: 146–49. doi:10.1038/382146a0

Kerrick, Derrill. M. 2001. *Present and Past Nonantropogenic CO₂ Degassing from the Solid Earth.* Reviews of Geophysics, 39 (4): 565–585. doi: 10.1029/2001rg000105

Kohlmaier, Gundolf H., H. Brohl, E.O. Sire, M. Plöchl and R. Revelle. 1987. *Modelling Stimulation of Plants and Ecosystem Response to the Present Levels of Excess Atmospheric CO₂.* Tellus, 39, Series B (Chemical and Physical Meteorology): 155–70.

Krajick, Kevin. 2005. *Fire in the Hole: Raging in Mines from Pennsylvania to China, Coal Fires Threaten Towns, Poison Air and Water, and Add to Global Warming.* Smithsonian Magazine, May 2005.

Lamb, Hubert. H. 1972. *Climate: Present, Past, and Future.* United Kingdom: Methuen Publishers.

Lamb, Hubert. H. 1995. *Climate, History, and the Modern World.* United Kingdom: Routledge.

LaViolette, Paul A. 2011. *Evidence for a Solar Flare Cause of the Pleistocene Mass Extinction.* Radiocarbon, 53 (2): 303–323.

Lawlor, D. W., and R. A. C. Mitchell. 1991. *The Effects of Increasing CO₂ on Crop Photosynthesis and Productivity: A Review of Field Studies.* Plant, Cell, & Environment, 14 (8): 807–18.

Leakey, Andrew D. 2009. *Rising Atmospheric Carbon Dioxide Concentration and the Future of C₄ Crops for Food and Fuel.* Proceedings of the Royal Society, B, 276 (1666): 2333–2243. doi: 10.1098/rspb.2008.1517

Lehmann, D. C. et al. 2003. *Amazonian Dark Earths: Origins, Properties, Management*. Netherlands: Kluwer Academic Publishers.

Lehmann, Johannes, B. Glaser, W.I. Woods, D.C. Kern (eds). 2003. *Amazonian Dark Earths: origin, properties, and management*. Dordrecht, The Netherlands. Kluwer.

Levine, Joel S., Bobbe, T., Ray, N., Singh, A. and R.G. Witt. 1999. *Wildland Fires and the Environment: a Global Synthesis*. United Nations Environmental Programme. UNEP/DEIAEW/TR.9–1.

Lewis, Simon L. et al. 2009. *Increasing Carbon Storage in Intact African Tropical Forests*. Nature, 457: 1003–1006. doi:10.1038/nature07771

Liu, Yi, Weiguo Liu, Zicheng Peng, Yingkai Xiao, Gangjian Wei, Weidong Sun, Jianfeng He, Guijian Liu, Chen-Lin Chou. 2009. *Instability of seawater pH in the South China Sea during the mid-late Holocene: Evidence from boron isotopic composition of corals*. Geochimica et Cosmochimica Acta 73: 1264-1272. doi:10.1016/j.gca.2008.11.034

MacDonald, G. M., K.V. Kremenetski and D.W. Beilman l. 2008. *Climate Change and the Northern Russian Tree-Line Zone*. Philosophical Transactions. Royal Society, London, B: Biological Sciences, 363 (1501): 2285–2299. doi: 10.1098/rstb.2007.2200

MacPhee, Ross D. E., and A. Greenwood. 2013. *Infectious Disease, Endangerment, and Extinction.* International Journal of Evolutionary Biology. Article ID 571939, 9pp. doi:10.1155/2013/571939

Mayeux, H. S., H. B. Johnson, H. W. Polley, and S. R. Malone. 1997. *Yield of Wheat Across a Subambient Carbon Dioxide Gradient*. Global Change Biology, 3: 269–78.

McElwain, J. C., F. E. Mayle and D. J. Beerling. 2002. *Stomatal Evidence for a Decline of Atmospheric CO_2 Concentration During the Younger*

Dryas Stadial: A Comparison with Antarctic Ice Core Records. Journal of Quaternary Science, 17 (1): 21–29. doi: 10.1002/jqs.664

Mörner, N. A., and G. Etiope. 2002. *Cambrian Degassing from the Lithosphere.* Global and Planetary Change, 33: 185–203.

Mossman David J., G. Eigendorf, D.Tokaryk, F. Gauthier-Lafaye, K.D. Guckert, V. Melezhik and C.E.G. Farrow. 2003. *Testing of Fullerenes in Geologic Materials: Oklo Carbonaceous Substances, Karelian Shungites, Sudbury Black Tuff.* Geology, 31: 255–258. doi: 10.1130/0091-7613

Mossman David J., F. Gauthier-Lafaye and S. E. Jackson. 2005. *Black Shale, Organic Matter, Ore Genesis and Hydrocarbon Generation in the Paleoproterozoic Franceville Series, Gabon.* Precambrian Research, 137(3-4): 253–272. DOI: 10.1016/j.precamres.2005.03.005

Muller, Richard A., and G. J. MacDonald. 1995. *Glacial Cycles and Orbital Inclination.* Nature, 377 (107 – 108. doi:10.1038/377107b0

Munday, P. L., M. I. McCormick, and G. E. Nilsson. 2012. *Impact of Global Warming and Rising CO_2 Levels on Coral Reef Fishes: What Hope for the Future?* Journal of Experimental Biology, 15 (215): 3865–3873.

Nicolaus, B. J. 2005. *A Critical Review of the Function of Neuromelanin and an Attempt to Provide a Unified Theory.* Medical Hypotheses, 65 (4): 791–796.

Olsson, L., L. Eklundh, and J. Ardo. 2005. *A Recent Greening of the Sahel—Trends, Patterns, and Potential Causes.* Journal of Arid Environments, 63: 556–66.

Osborne, C. P., and D. J. Beerling. 2006. *Nature's Green Revolution: The Remarkable Evolutionary Rise of C_4 Plants.* Philosophical

Transactions Royal Society, London, B: Biological Sciences, 361 (1465): 173–194.

Pandolfi, J. M. 2011. *Projecting Coral Reef Futures Under Global Warming and Ocean Acidification*. Science, 333 (6041): 418–422.

Patterson, R. Timothy, A.P. Dalby, H.M. Roe, J.P. Guilbault, I. Hutchinson and J.J. Clague. 2005. *Relative Utility of Foraminifera, Diatoms, and Macrophytes as High Resolution Indicators of Paleo-Sea Level in coastal British Columbia, Canada*. Quaternary Science Reviews, 24(18-19): 2002–2014. doi: 10.1016/j.quascirev.2004.11.013

Pausas, Juli G., and J. E. Keely. 2009. *A Burning Story: The Role of Fire in the History of Life*. Bioscience, 59 (7): 593–601. doi: http://dx.doi.org/10.1525/bio.2009.59.7.10

Pearson, Richard G., S. J. Phillips, M.M. Loranty, P.S.A. Beck, T. Damoulas, S. J. Knight and S.J. Goetz. 2013. *Shifts in Arctic Vegetation and Associated Feedbacks Under Climate Change*. Nature Climate Change, 3: 673–677. doi:10.1038/nclimate1858

Pelejero C., E. Calvo, and O. Hoegh-Guldberg. 2010. *Paleo-Perspectives on Ocean Acidification*. Trends in Ecology & Evolution, 25 (6): 332–344.

Plimer, I. R. 2009. *Heaven and Earth: Global Warming, the Missing Science*. Connor Court Publishing, Australia. 504 pp.

Polley, Wayne H., H.B. Johnson and H.S. Mayeux. 1992. *Carbon Dioxide and Water Fluxes of C_3 Annuals and C_3 and C_4 Perennials at Subambient CO_2 Concentrations*. Functional Ecology 6: 693-703

Polley, Wayne H., H.B. Johnson, B.D. Marinot and H.S. Mayeux. 1993. *Increase in C3 plant water-use efficiency and biomass over Glacial to present C02 concentrations*. Nature 361, 61 - 64; doi:10.1038/361061a0

Poorter, Hendrik. 1993. *Interspecific Variation in the Growth Response of Plants to an Elevated Ambient CO_2 Concentration.* Vegetatio, 104 (105): 77–97.

Poorter, Hendrik, and M. Perez-Soba. 2001. *The Growth Response of Plants to Elevated CO_2 Under Non-Optimal Environmental Conditions.* Oecologia, 129: 1–20.

Pyne, Steven J. 2001. *Fire: A Brief History (Cycle of Fire).* Seattle: University of Washington Press. 204pp.

Quinton, René. 1904. *L'eau de Mer, Milieu Organique.* Paris: Masson, Editions Encre.

Rasool, Ichtiaque S. and S. H. Schneider. 1971. *Atmospheric Carbon Dioxide and Aerosols: Effects of Large Increases on Global Climate.* Science, 173: 138–41. doi:10.1126/science.173.3992.138

Reeves, Timothy G. (2012) *Australian Grains Free Air CO2 Enrichment (AGFACE).* PICCC Annual Report (2011/2012). The University of Melbourne, Australia

Roberts, W. O., and R. H. Olson. 1973. *New Evidence for Effects of Variable Solar Corpuscular Emission on the Weather.* Reviews of Geophysics, 11 (3): 731–40.

Rogier de Jong, Jan Verbesselt, M. E. Schaepman and Sytze de Bruinl. 2011. *Trend Changes in Global Greening and Browning: Contribution of Short-Term Trends to Longer-Term Change.* Global Change Biology, 18 (2): 642–55. doi: 10.1111/j.1365-2486.2011.02578.x

Roosevelt, A. 2013. *Prehistory of Amazonia in Cambridge World Prehistory.* Edited by Colin Renfrew and Paul Bahn. Cambridge, UK: Cambridge University Press.

Royer, Dana L. 2006. *CO₂-Forced Climate Thresholds during the Phanerozoic* Geochimica et Cosmochimica Acta, 70 (23): 5665–75. doi: 10.1016/j.gca.2005.11.031

Sage, Rowan F. 1995. *Was Low Atmospheric CO_2 During the Pleistocene a Limiting Factor for the Origin of Agriculture?* Global Change Biology, 1 (2): 93–106. doi: 10.1111/j.1365-2486.1995.tb00009.x

Sampath, S., T.K. Abraham, V. Sasi Kumar and C.N. Mohanan. 2001. *Coloured Rain: a report on the phenomenon.* Tropical Botanic Garden and Research Institute. Centre for Earth Science Studies. Trivandrum, Kerala, India

Scheiter, S., and S. I. Higgins. 2009. *Impacts of Climate Change on the Vegetation of Africa: An Adaptive Dynamic Vegetation Modeling Approach.* Global Change Biology, 15: 2224–46.

Seaquist, J. W., L. Olsson, J. Ardo and L. Eklundh. 2006. *Broad-Scale Increase in NPP Quantified for the African Sahel, 1982–1999.* International Journal of Remote Sensing, 27: 5115–5122.

Shaviv, N. J., and J. Veizer. 2003. *Celestial Driver of Phanerozoic Climate?* Geological Society of America Today, 13 (7): 4–10.

Stratcher, G. B. 2007. *Geology of Coal Fires: Case Studies from Around the World.* IN Reviews in Engineering Geology, XVIII. Geological Society of America.

Stracher, G.B., A. Prakash, and E. V. Sokol, E. V. 2011. *Coal and Peat Fires: A Global Perspective.* Edited by Elsevier B. V.

Stretch, R. C., and H. A. Viles. 2002. *The Nature and Rate of Weathering by Lichens on Lava Flows on Lanzarote.* Geomorphology, 47 (1): 87–94.

The Royal Society (Chair Prof. John Raven). 2005. *Ocean Acidification Due to Increasing Carbon Dioxide.* Policy Document 12/05

Thoning, K. W., P. P. Tans, and W. D. Komhyr, 1989. *Atmospheric Carbon Dioxide at Mauna Loa Observatory 2. Analysis of the NOAA GMCC Data, 1974–1985.* Journal of Geophysical Research-Atmospheres, 94 (6): 8549–65.

Trenberth, Kevin E., A. Dai, G. van der Schrier, P.D. Jones, J. Barichivich, K.R. Briffaand, J. Sheffield. 2014. *Global Warming and Changes in Drought.* Nature Climate Change, 4: 17–22. doi:10.1038/nclimate2067

Tripati, Aradhna K., C.D. Roberts and R.A. Eagle. 2009. *Coupling of CO_2 and Ice Sheet Stability Over Major Climate Transitions of the Last 20 Million Years.* Science, 326(5958): 1394–1397. doi: 10.1126/science.1178296

Van Dijk, Paul, J. Zhang, W. Jun, C. Kuenzer, K.-H. Wolf (2011) *Applications of Remote Sensing and GIS for Monitoring of Coal Fires, Mine Subsidence, Environmental Impacts of Coal-Mine Closure and Reclamation. Pages 108-119 IN Assessment of the contribution of in-situ combustion of coal to greenhouse gas emission; based on a comparison of Chinese mining information to previous remote sensing estimates.* International Journal of Coal Geology, 86 (1): 1–120 (Articles 1 – 14)

Veron, John E. N. 2008. *Mass Extinctions and Ocean Acidification: Biological Constraints on Geological Dilemmas.* Coral Reefs, 27 (3): 459–72. Doi: 10.1007/s00338-008-0381-8

Wagner, Friederike, L.L.R. Kouwenberg, T.B. van Hoof and H. Visscher. 2004. *Reproducibility of Holocene Atmosphere CO_2 Records Based on Stomatal Frequency.* Quaternary Science Reviews, 23: 1947–1954.

Wang, J., H. W. Pfefferkorn, Y. Zang, and Z. Feng. 2012. *Permian Vegetacional Pompeii from Inner Mongolia and its Implications for*

Landscape Paleoecology and Paleobiogeography of Cathaysia. Proceedings of the National Academy of Sciences USA, 109 (13): 4927–4932.

Wang, S. Y., J. A. Bunce, and J. L. Maas. 2003. *Elevated Carbon Dioxide Increases Contents of Antioxidant Compounds in Field-Grown Strawberries.* Journal of Agricultural and Food Chemistry 16 (51): 4315–4320.

Wang, Xuhui. et al. 2014. *A Two-Fold Increase of Carbon Cycle Sensitivity to Tropical Temperature Variations..* Nature 506: 212–215. doi:10.1038/nature12915

Warren, J. K. 2006. *Evaporites: Sediments, Resources, and Hydrocarbons.* 1036pp. Springer, New York. 2006 edition

Warren, J. K., S.C. George, P.J. Hamilton and P. Tingate. 1998. *Proterozoic Source Rocks: Sedimentology and Organic Characteristics of the Velkerri Formation, Northern Territory, Australia.* American Association of Petroleum Geologists Bulletin, 82 (3): 442–463.

Wood, R. A., J.P. Grotzinger and J.A. Dickson. 2002. *Proterozoic Modular Biomineralized Metazoan from the Nama Group, Namibia.* Science, 296 (5577): 2383–2386. PMID: 12089440

Xu, L. et al. 2013. *Temperature and Vegetation Seasonality Diminishment over Northern Lands.* Nature Climate Change, 3: 581–586. doi:10.1038/nclimate1836

ABOUT THE AUTHOR

Juan Carlos Mirre is a geologist who graduated from the Universidad de Buenos Aires (Argentina) with an MSc degree and a Masters in Economic Geology from the Sorbonne University (Paris, France). During his professional life, he was in charge of numerous projects as an exploration geologist in many countries in South America, Europe, and Western Asia. He was also involved in a number of studies concerning the environmental impact assessment of development and operation projects. He is also an author of both scientific papers and science for general audience, articles and books, mostly written in Spanish. J.C. Mirre is also a private tutor for masters and graduate degree students in economics and applied geology.

His book, *The "Peak Oil" Myth Debunked: There Is Plenty of Oil for Another Century,* was published by Amazon Books in 2014.

Printed in Great Britain
by Amazon